D1499305

Art in Context

J. L. David: Brutus

Art in Context

Edited by John Fleming and Hugh Honour

Each volume in this series discusses a famous painting or sculpture as both image and idea in its context – whether stylistic, technical, literary, psychological, religious, social or political. In what circumstances was it conceived and created? What did the artist hope to achieve? What means did he employ, subconscious or conscious? Did he succeed? Or how far did he succeed? His preparatory drawings and sketches often allow us some insight into the creative process and other artists' renderings of the same or similar themes help us to understand his problems and ambitions. Technique and his handling of the medium are fascinating to watch close up. And the work's impact on contemporaries and its later influence on other artists can illuminate its meaning for us today.

By focusing on these outstanding paintings and sculptures our understanding of the artist and the world in which he lived is sharpened. But since all great works of art are unique and every one presents individual problems of understanding and appreciation, the authors of these volumes emphasize whichever aspects seem most relevant. And many great masterpieces, too often and too easily accepted and dismissed because they have become familiar, are shown to contain further and deeper layers of meaning for us.

Art in Context

Jacques-Louis David was born to a prosperous middle-class family in Paris on 30 August 1748. His training was in the highly stratified system of the Royal Academy, where his chief teacher (from 1766) was Joseph Vien. The Prix de Rome finally took him to Italy in 1775, and he slowly developed the vigorous neo-classical manner which was declared in his Oath of the Horatii *(1785). This picture,* Socrates *(1787) and* Brutus *(1789) made him France's leading painter, and in the Revolution he assumed a major political role as well. His paintings of the martyrs* Marat *and* Lepeletier *in 1793 were essential elements of his public role, as were the great festivals he helped design. He continued to paint portraits throughout this period and stands among the greatest of French portraitists. David forsook active politics after the fall of Robespierre, but as artist and teacher he was a major figure in the Napoleonic era. He was exiled by the restoration government in 1815, and spent the last decade of his active life in Brussels, where he died on 29 December 1825.*

Lictors Returning to Brutus the Bodies of his Sons, painted in oil on canvas (325 x 423 cm.) was first conceived in 1787, and completed during the first summer of the Revolution for exhibition at the Salon in September, 1789. It is now in the Louvre. Records survive of many drawings for the huge canvas, but only one oil sketch and a handful of drawings can now be located. Several reduced copies of the picture, probably due to David's pupils, are presently in public and private collections in Paris, Besançon, Warsaw and Hartford, Connecticut.

Allen Lane The Penguin Press

David, Voltaire, **Brutus** *and the French Revolution:*
an essay in art and politics

Robert L. Herbert

Copyright © Robert L. Herbert, 1972
First published in 1972
Allen Lane The Penguin Press, 74 Grosvenor Street, London W1
ISBN 0 7139 0278 7
Filmset in Monophoto Ehrhardt by Oliver Burridge Filmsetting Ltd, Crawley, England
Color plate printed photogravure by D. H. Greaves Ltd, Scarborough, England
Printed and bound by W. & J. Mackay & Co. Ltd, Chatham, England

Designed by Gerald Cinamon and Veronica Loveless

To EWH

Reference color plate at end of book

Acknowledgments

This study began in 1955 as part of a graduate course at Yale under the guidance of John McCoubrey, and was encouraged by my admiration for the work of Jean Locquin, Jules Renouvier, F. A. Aulard, David Dowd and Robert Rosenblum. I have benefited especially from my wife's judgment of historical issues, and I am grateful for the comments and advice of Robert Lopez, Pierre Rosenberg and Peter Walch. Students in the several courses into which I have introduced these materials have offered the invaluable service of assisting in the process of sorting out major elements from minor ones. For help in obtaining photographs and documents, I gladly list my debts to Jan Bialostocki, Per Bjurstroem, Vivian Cameron, Jacques Foucart, Jean-Marie Girard, Lucy Grace, Thomas Greene and Carlos Van Hasselt. My colleagues at the Louvre, Michel Laclotte, Pierre Rosenberg and Jacques Foucart were particularly generous and forebearing, as were also Jean-Marie Girard at Tours, Jean Adhémar of the Cabinet des Estampes, and Jacques Wilhelm and the staff of the Musée Carnavalet. John Fleming has offered editorial advice with the eye of a falcon and the tact of an Eastern diplomat. All translations are my own unless otherwise noted, and I have modernized spellings in both English and French. I was restrained from broad generalizations about revolutionary art and neoclassicism by the limitations of space and by a laudable portion of cowardice.

RLH
June 1971

Historical Table

1787 Calonne's financial reforms rejected (May). Louis XVI convokes States General for 1792.

1788 Louis XVI summons States General for May 1789. Brienne announces national bankruptcy; Necker recalled.

1789 States General meet at Versailles (May). Third Estate constitutes itself as National Assembly to prepare a new constitution; Tennis Court Oath (June). Bastille assaulted (July). Declarations of Rights of Man and Citizen (Aug.). The Great Fear in the provinces (July–Aug.). Women march on Versailles (Oct.). Church property nationalized (Nov.).

1790 Festival of Unity, Louis XVI accepts constitution (July). Civil constitution of clergy (July).

1791 Mirabeau President of Assembly (Jan.); dies (April). Louis XVI captured at Varennes while fleeing (June). Festival honoring Voltaire (July). Constitution passed by Assembly (Sept.).

1792 Festival of Liberty (April). War declared on Austria (April) and Prussia (July), who invade France. Assault on Tuileries, royal family imprisoned (Aug.). French victory at Valmy, and Republic proclaimed (Sept.).

1793 Louis XVI executed (Jan.). First Coalition against France by Britain, Austria, Prussia, Holland, Spain, Sardinia (Feb.). Revolt in La Vendée (March). Committee of Public Safety formed (April). Girondists overthrown, Terror begins (June). Marat assassinated (July). Marie-Antoinette executed (Oct.). Levy of male population (Aug.). Substantial military victories (Oct.–Dec.); Napoleon retakes Toulon (Dec.).

1794 Executions of Hébertists (Mar.) and Dantonists (April). Festival of Supreme Being (June). Fall of Robespierre (July). Readmission of Girondists to Convention (Dec.).

Salon: David's *Death of Socrates*. Canova begins *Tomb of Clement XIII*. Flaxman goes to Rome.

J. J. Barthélemy, *Voyage du jeune Anarcharsis en Grèce*. A. L. Lavoisier, *Méthode de nomenclature chimique*. Mozart, *Don Giovanni*. — 1787

David's *Lavoisier and his Wife*. Death of Gainsborough.

Lemprière, *Classical Dictionary*. Kant, *Critique of Practical Reason*. Alfieri, *Bruto Primo*. — 1788

Salon: **David's *Brutus***, and *Paris and Helen*; Robin's *Lally-Tollendal Unveiling the Bust of his Father*; Peyron's *Death of Socrates*; Houdon's *Washington*. Goya named Painter of the Royal Household. Death of Joseph Vernet. Blake's *Songs of Innocence*.

Bernardin de St Pierre, *Paul et Virginie*. M.-J. Chénier, *Charles IX*. E. J. Sieyès, *Qu'est-ce que le Tiers Etat?* and *Exposition des Droits de l'homme*. Completion of 70-volume Kehl edition of Voltaire's works. — 1789

David lionized in Nantes (April).

Burke, *Reflexions on the French Revolution*. A. Chénier, *Avis de peuple français* and *Jeu de Paume*. Voltaire's *Brutus* revived (Nov). — 1790

Salon: David's drawing of *Oath in Tennis Court*; his earlier pictures *Horatii*, *Socrates* and *Brutus*. Birth of Géricault.

T. Paine, *Rights of Man*, I (completed 1792). Marquis de Sade, *Justine*. Volney, *Les Ruines*. M.-J. Chénier, *Jean Calas*. Talma's secessionist Théâtre de la Rue de Richelieu. — 1791

David elected Deputy to Convention (Sept); named to Committee of Public Instruction (Oct). Deaths of Robert Adam and Joshua Reynolds.

Mary Wollstonecroft, *Rights of Women*. J. B. (Anarchis) Cloots, *La République Universelle*. C. J. Rouget de Lisle, *La Marseillaise*. — 1792

Salon: Girodet's *Endymion*. David President of Jacobins (June–July); offers his paintings of martyred *Lepeletier* and *Marat* to the Convention; named to Committee of Public Safety (Sept). Convention decree abolishes Académie (Aug).

Condorcet, *Tableau de Progrès de l'esprit humain*. Cloots, *Base constitutionelle de la république du genre humain*. — 1793

David presides over Convention (Jan); leaves *The Young Martyr Bara* in unfinished state; imprisoned after fall of Robespierre, released 1795. Blake's *First Book of Urizen*. Flaxman returns from Rome.

S. T. Coleridge and R. Southey, *The Fall of Robespierre*. — 1794

1. David's Painting of Brutus

One of the most extraordinary events ever to bring art into the focus of political action took place in Paris in November 1790, sixteen months after the fall of the Bastille and fourteen after Jacques-Louis David had exhibited his new painting of *Brutus* [Color Plate]. On 17 and 19 November 1790, there were the first two presentations of a revival of Voltaire's *Brutus* at the National Theatre. 'This play, in which the horror of a tyrannical government is expressed with all the fire of Voltaire's genius . . ., had attracted to its first representation both those whose thought has been elevated by our fortunate Revolution, and also those whose pride has been humbled by it.'[1] The royalists in the audience applauded those lines favoring Tarquin, and the radicals, those favoring Brutus and the Roman republic. The republicans were in better voice and their spokesmen in the press made clear their identification with the republic of Rome: 'Never was illusion more complete: the spectators were as so many Romans; all believed they were participating in the action.'[2] When Brutus cried 'Gods! Give us death rather than slavery!', the applause and shouts were so deafening and the dust so thick that several moments were needed to restore order.

On the second night, the royalists having been cowed, the audience seemed exclusively pro-republican. David, who had extensive friendships in the theatre, placed on one side of the stage a copy of the bronze bust of Brutus which he had brought back from Rome, and on the other, Voltaire's bust by Houdon. Various homages were offered to the ancient and to the modern hero. At the end of the play, 'they put into action the painting by David. At the moment when the death of his son is announced to Brutus, this unfortunate father seats himself in an antique chair, like the artist's Brutus, and in the same fashion one sees going past the funeral cortège which carried the two sons back to the house.'[3]

From that point forward, David, Voltaire and the figure of Brutus were thoroughly intertwined in the events of the Revolution. David was one of the principal organizers of the national homage to Voltaire in July 1791, during which citations from his *Brutus* were given prominence. The play became a staple of the Revolution, and a contemporary bust of Brutus was placed before the speakers' rostrum in the National Convention. The particular fascination in studying this phenomenon lies in the fact that David's painting, like Voltaire's play, was composed without reference to the revolutionary implications of the theme. It was the events of 1789 to 1794 which redefined the painting and the play, and this transformation is the subject of the present study.

The story of Lucius Junius Brutus, who lived five hundred years before Caesar's assassin Marcus Brutus,[4] begins with the rise to power of the last king of Rome, Tarquin the Proud. Tarquin and his wife Tullia had murdered their first mates to be free to marry one another, and then Tarquin killed the king, his new wife's father. The usurper put many senators to death and ruled autocratically. He also murdered most of the family of Brutus, his nephew, who survived in the royal household by feigning stupidity (brutishness – hence the name Brutus).

This dissolute monarchy came to an end when Tarquin's son Sextus raped the virtuous Lucretia, the wife of Collatinus. She called together her father and her husband, who came accompanied by Publius Valerius and Brutus, and stabbed herself in their presence to expiate the stain. Brutus suddenly revealed his true nature by drawing the knife from the fatal wound and swearing on Lucretia's blood to rid Rome of the Tarquins and of the very institution of monarchy. He then had the other three men swear the same oath over the knife, and later in public bound the populace to it as well. Brutus then led the successful fight against Tarquin, and the royal family was exiled. The first Roman republic was established (508 B.C.) with Brutus and Collatinus elected co-consuls. It is at this point that Livy began his Book II (Baker edition) with the memorable words 'Henceforward I am to treat of the affairs, civil and military, of a free people, for such the Romans were now become; of annual magistrates, and the authority of the laws exalted above that of man.'

These events would undoubtedly have sufficed to give Brutus adequate fame, but he performed another act so terrifying in its devotion to the state that it became the central element of his legend. His two adolescent sons, Titus and Tiberius, were drawn into a royalist conspiracy by their mother's family, the Vitelii, and Brutus was obliged to order and to witness their execution. Livy merely comments that at the execution 'the looks and countenance of Brutus afforded an extraordinary spectacle, the feelings of the father often struggling with the character of the magistrate', but Plutarch (Clough/Dryden edition) was more disturbed.

'Brutus . . . is said not to have turned aside his face, nor allowed the least glance of pity to soften and smooth his aspect of rigor and austerity, but sternly watched his children suffer . . . An action truly open alike to the highest commendation and the strongest censure; for either the greatness of his virtue raised him above the impressions of sorrow, or the extravagance of his misery took away all sense of it; but neither seemed common, or the result of humanity, but either divine or brutish.'

This nearly inhuman act of sacrifice of one's blood to the state was a worthy challenge to both writer and painter. Brutus's earlier act, the oath over Lucretia's body, is more or less readily imagined, but writers had to invent all manner of circumstance to make Brutus's later action believable. David, as we are about to see, was led to invent a scene never before part of the legend in order to deal with Brutus's agony.

The origins of David's *Brutus* go back to 1787, two years after he had been catapulted to fame by the exhibition of his *Oath of the Horatii* [1]. He was asked to submit subjects for a government commission for the Salon of 1787. This was a way of subsidizing the more notable artists who, like David, were associated or full members of the Academy of Fine Arts, and who had been brought along in the state system with many fellowships and awards. David now proposed two subjects: Coriolanus restrained by his family from seeking revenge, and the departure of Attilius Regulus.[5] The first of these was accepted by the Comte d'Angiviller, Superintendent of Fine Arts, but there is no surviving record of drawings for a Coriolanus, although David's posthumous sale did list two drawings of the *Departure of Attilius Regulus*. The commission was not fulfilled in 1787, and in early 1789, as official correspondence reveals, the state still assumed that David was preparing a Coriolanus for the Salon. The artist had simply substituted *Brutus* for Coriolanus without informing the royal commissioners, probably confident that his fame would guarantee government purchase. When we come to the events of 1789, we shall reexamine the 'republican' theme of Brutus versus the 'monarchist' one of Coriolanus, in order to see if nascent republican sentiment helped determine David's choice.

In his eventual claim for payment, David said that *Brutus* was done in 1788 and 1789, but a drawing often described in the nineteenth century, subsequently lost from sight, was apparently done in 1787. 'The two consuls are seated on a tribune in front of a temple. Collatinus covers his face, but Brutus looks upon the execution with a sober eye. His sons have already been seized by the lictors, and one of them, on his knees by the executioner's block, implores his father's pity. In the left background others of the guilty are being led in. In front, the column to which the condemned are bound.'[6]

This makes it nearly certain that David began with the execution scene which was, along with the oath over Lucretia's body, the

1. *The Oath of the Horatii*, 1784–5. David.

usual choice from the Brutus story and which, since the middle of the century, had been favored as an example of heroic virtue.[7] But David was seldom satisfied with the ordinary treatment of a theme. His *Oath of the Horatii* was already a notable instance of invention, and his change to the new Brutus scene was consistent with his instinct for drama of tension rather than for overt action.

In the first of the surviving drawings [2] Brutus is not the consul witnessing a public event, conscious that everyone's eye is on him, but the father, slumped in dejection. In the next [3], Brutus's pose is considerably altered. The legs are both drawn back, one arm

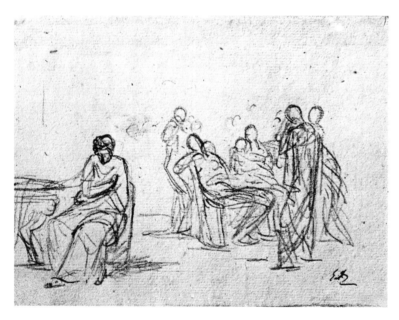

2 (*left*). *Brutus and his Household*, *c*. 1788. David.

3 (*below*). *The Dejected Brutus*, *c*. 1788. David.

dangles down, and the other is drawn over a faint upraised arm which is being temporarily set aside as a solution. The third drawing [4] at the outset had Brutus's head in the position of dejection (it shows to the right of the darker head), but this was changed to the erect pose of the final picture. David has thought his way further into the story, and the erect head is a response to Brutus's reverie being interrupted, a change paralleled by the shift from

4. Compositional study for
Brutus, c. 1788. David.

the passive group of the first drawing [2] to the active one of this
version. Here the figures, in which we now recognize Brutus's
wife and daughters, are aroused at the sight of the sons' bodies.
The empty chair is a sign that the former passive state is over.

The third drawing has the complexity of David's rather baroque
early works, such as his *Antiochus and Stratonice* (École des Beaux-
Arts) of 1774. A vaulted corridor slants away at the extreme left

and the bearers are moving into an atrium, with subsidiary space openings to the rear. Columns left and right (the figures leaning into the composition between the far right columns echo Raphael-esque recipes) divide the space in a rather unclear way. This complexity will be greatly reduced in the finished picture, an evolution typical of David's *Horatii* and other works, in which the maturing of one composition seems to recapitulate the artist's whole process of shifting from the early baroque style to his fully fledged neo-classical manner, as though the youth of the composition were an equivalent of the youth of the artist.

In the bottom fragment of the next drawing [5], the group of mother and daughters is unchanged, but in the whole study above, one daughter shifts toward her final definition by clinging to her

5 (*left*). *Brutus's Wife and Daughters*, *c.* 1788. David.

6 (*above*). Illustration for Voltaire's *Irène*, 1786.

7 (*right*). Compositional study for *Brutus*, *c.* 1788. David.

mother in a near faint. In the earlier poses of this group, the women seemed to react each in the same way and the daughters could be imagined as assisting their mother. Now she begins to acquire the protective role she eventually assumes. At this point, her pose, taken alone, is close enough to that of Moreau-le-Jeune's engraving for Voltaire's *Irène* [6] to remind us that stage conventions undoubtedly entered, if only unconsciously, into David's processes. The engraving of 1786 seems to reflect the actual staging of Voltaire's plays which were notably 'classical', and might have had an effect on the painter, who was an intimate of the theatre.

The fainting daughter has her head back and comes still closer to the oil painting in the fifth drawing [7]. Brutus's pose has not altered much compared with the Lehman study [4], but the column

behind him has been shifted to the left, bringing the sons' bodies into more immediate proximity to him. In *Brutus seated, head erect* [8] the feet are reversed, the head has a more noble aspect, and the chair is at last that of the oil painting, and identical with that of the *Seated Philosopher* which David had drawn in the Villa Negroni collection in Rome.[8] The chair has become progressively more prominent in this succession of drawings. It now pushes out laterally to the right to span the gap between Brutus and that side of the composition, and to make obvious Brutus's tense position on the edge of his seat. Between this drawing and the oil sketch in Stockholm [10], there survives only the tiny drawing of the weeping servant [9]. There must have been many others, because the oil

8 (*left*). *Brutus seated,* *c.* 1788. David.

9 (*right*). Study for *Weeping Servant,* *c.* 1788. David.

sketch contains all the major elements of the Louvre painting, and these would have been worked out in preparatory drawings.

After the oil sketch came the little drawing of the fainting daughter which David put in his letter to Wicar [11], and the most polished of the known drawings for *Brutus*, and one of the handsomest of all of David's drawings, the *Weeping Servant* [13]. The general position of the servant was established in the oil sketch,

10. Study for *Brutus*, *c.* 1788. David.

but David decided to mask her with a long sweep of blue drapery. Had he retained the figure as in the sketch, the varied movements of her body would have given that part of the picture too much three-dimensional activity. He also eliminated the statue above, so that the plane of the drapery behind would work with the lateral and rising plane of the servant's cloth to create a flattened and simplified area.[9] Another function of the curve of the servant's costume [14] is to echo the opposed curve of the isolated chair in the middle of the picture. Together the two form a cupped frame for the pyramidal cluster of women.

The only other known drawing for Brutus is the previously unidentified study [12] for the mother's foot and skirt. It is on a page of a sketchbook otherwise devoted to classical art, apparently dating from David's second Roman trip of 1784-5, and is tangible proof that the artist went back over his notebook while finishing the 1789 picture. The drawing is nearly identical with the definitive form, but the sandal is lacking, and there is no indication of the final drop of the undergarment down to floor level. In fact, the flap to our left in the drawing folds back, implying a continuous

11. *The Fainting Daughter*, 1789. David.

12 (*right*). Study for *Brutus*, *c.* 1789. David.

ground plane. This may mean that the little fragment was done after a precise model, and modified in the ultimate composition. It might seem unlikely that the artist would incorporate a literal copy in his painting, and yet remarkably similar examples of the projecting nude foot and flowing skirt can be found in crouching Niobid sculptures, including one David drew,[10] as well as in dancing figures from antiquity.

That David consulted Roman sculpture is of course clear. His notebooks served as galleries of motifs and poses, and he also used published repertoria. Sometimes his care in seeking the sanction of a classical prototype seems excessive. In his letter of 14 June 1789 to Wicar, he enclosed the ink sketches [11] of the fainting

13. *The Weeping Servant,*
1789. David.

14 (*right*). Detail from *Brutus,*
1789. David.

daughter and asked his pupil 'to sketch for me on this [illegible]
head a coiffure in the position I indicate. It seems to me that you
will probably find it among the Bacchanales. One often sees
Bacchantes with this sort of pose. However, no matter as long as
you send me a dishevelled coiffure of a young girl, a period coiffure.
Do not try to make a finished drawing, I will not take advantage of
you that much. Besides, I only need enough lines to distinguish
well all the masses of the hair.'[11] In fact, however, David hardly
needed such help because the little sketch on the right shows all
the essential dispositions of the hair as finally painted, and his
Roman notebooks contained a number of appropriate coiffures.

What is especially instructive in the request to Wicar is the reference to bacchantes. They are often shown in classical sculpture with their heads thrown back in ecstasy, their bodies undulating and knees deeply bent, very much like David's swooning girl [17]. This pose was widespread in Roman art and was also used for displays of hysterical grief.[12] We should not, therefore, be surprised that joy and despair could be embodied in similar poses. It was David's contemporary Sir Joshua Reynolds who, citing a bac-

15. The Capitoline *Brutus*.

chante's joy and a Magdalen's grief, remarked that 'It is curious to observe, and it is certainly true, that the extremes of passions are, with very little variation, expressed by the same action.'[13]

Antique sources for *Brutus* have been largely summarized by Louis Hautecoeur,[14] but a few nuances can be supplied. Brutus's head is from the Capitoline bust [15] of which David owned a copy, and of which he had earlier traced a profile view [16]. The tracing is David's first known contact with the famous antique personage.

16. The Capitoline *Brutus,*
c. 1784? David.

Brutus's pose is a combination of several Roman sculptures of seated figures, but the statue of Rome comes from the famous Montfaucon[15] and not from the Capitoline. The litter bearers are not close enough to the Arch of Titus to warrant Hautecoeur's claim that it is the source. The origin of the apparently true anecdote that the furniture was actually made by the famous Jacob following David's instructions is the reliable Delécluze. It is Delécluze also who said that in the dimly seen relief of Romulus and Remus on the pedestal of *Roma*, David was trying to re-create what he imagined to be crude sculpture of early Rome. It can now be shown that this painted relief is a combination of the Etruscan bronze group in the Capitoline and another Romulus and Remus group, this time a bas-relief in the Vatican which David sketched in the later Roman notebook.[16] The banded hairdo of the upright daughter is the same as that on a pencil drawing of the Roman period,[17] and her swirling garment is very close to those frequently found on dancing figures, such as the reliefs of dancers in the Villa Medici and in the Uffizi, widely published in David's time.

We come closer to the actual expression of the group of women when we consider their most important Roman prototype, the Niobids. Reliefs devoted to the theme frequently include a mother with two children clinging to her. The sarcophagus in the Lateran [18] has such a group on the right, with one daughter in a position quite like that of the Bayonne study [7]. The Vatican Niobids [19] include a group in which one child is fainting, and the other holding up a hand in horror, in these ways foretelling the roles of David's two girls.[18] The appropriateness of the theme, of course, is that Niobe has to witness the slaying of her children by the gods, and Brutus's wife and daughters have to see the sons' bodies being returned. In addition, there is perhaps a latent connection: Niobe's children were slain by the gods because she boasted of their beauty, a punishment of pride that seems to lie behind the execution of the Roman consul's own children.[19]

17. *Brutus*, detail.

18 (*above*). Niobid Sarcophagus, detail.

19 (*above right*). Niobid Sarcophagus, detail.

The consul himself in David's painting is partly based on the antique figure commonly called the 'seated philosopher'. When in Rome, David had drawn more than one such statue, including one then in the Villa Negroni whose chair and simple footstool are retained in the final composition, as is the fall of drapery over the seat cushion. In another one, from the Giustiniani collection,[20] the pose is close to the earliest surviving idea for David's Brutus [2]. The closest of all to the expression of the figure is not included in the artist's surviving drawings, but it was in a famous collection and he had certainly seen it: the brooding figure from the Palazzo Spada [20].

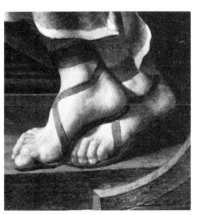

20. *Seated Philosopher*.

21. *Brutus*, detail.

None of these sculptures has the raised hand of David's Brutus nor his crossed feet [21], two of the artist's most essential and revealing inventions. The crossed feet might be an echo of the sad or soulful position of seated figures with one knee crossed over the other.[21] The raised arm, however, has important classical antecedents. The Vatican's famous *Penelope*, seated with her legs crossed, has her right elbow on her knee, and her raised hand almost touching her head. More common in Roman art is the gesture of raised forearm, at a modest distance from the head, which is usually indicative of a command to attention while the figure speaks. The most interesting of these for David is the one he traced from a book [22][22] in which

22. *Jupiter, c.* 1784? David.

a seated Jupiter has this gesture, although the forearm is a bit further from the head.

David arrived at this solution in order to shift his chief actor from a pensive pose, where the hand touched the head, to one in which he asserts a kind of stern anger at being brought suddenly out of his painful meditation. The essential idea for it came from Michelangelo. In his letter about *Brutus* to Wicar of June 1789 (see Appendix), David mentioned Michelangelo just before speaking of the basic qualities of 'feeling and composition', and in the second letter, which talks of the public reception of the picture, he is obviously pleased that contemporaries saw 'something of Florence in the form of my Brutus'. What David sought, and contemporaries admired, was the somber force, the tragic power of the great Renaissance master, and this general effect was seconded by the echo of the pose of Isaiah, one of Michelangelo's prophets on the Sistine ceiling [23]. Isaiah has been roused from his meditation by a cherub. His feet are crossed and one hand holds a book of his writings, indications of his prior state of intense meditation. His response to the interruption is found in the erect head and the upraised hand and arm. There is little doubt that the Italian master showed David how bodily position and movement could embody diverse emotional qualities in one figure. Of course the strong internal oppositions of Michelangelo's figure are developed in a spiral of spatial movement, whereas Brutus has been pressed flatly onto the surface plane. David must have thought that this was 'correcting' Michelangelo by a greater attention to classical art.

We should not forget that in David's time, originality was invested in the added dimension given to an already famous theme. It was the highest calling to challenge great art of the past by taking up its themes – and surpassing them. The excavations at Pompeii and Herculaneum in the middle of the century and the many sculptures unearthed in Rome had shown artists the immense variety and richness of antique art. The classical tradition which was so basic a part of a French artist's training had become rather enervated, and

23. *Isaiah*. Michelangelo.

had been passed on by the teachers more through their own late baroque manner than through original study of the objects themselves. David's contribution was to go directly back to antique art, to insist upon a detailed knowledge of its extraordinary resources, and at the same time to go directly to the study of natural form itself. Classical poses and motifs were studied, yes, but as a base upon which a new art was built. One of our sorest regrets must be the loss of most of the drawings for *Brutus*, drawings like the *Weeping Servant* [13], the only one which shows the application of David's tensile vision to the live model.

For it is this taut, astricted vision which is David's own, and which reaches through the large canvas, stretching the membrane of paint tightly over the minimum number of images. Individual motifs are not as important as the control over them. The opposite is true of the work of talented, but lesser men. J. F. P. Peyron's *Death of Socrates* [24] hung on the same wall with *Brutus* in the

24. *Death of Socrates.*
Engraving. 1790.
J. F. P. Peyron.

Salon of 1789. It also represents a break with the swirling movement of the rococo style of the preceding generation. But it seems too patently contrived when compared to David, too concerned with individual motifs, with the *beaux morceaux* of the studio.

David's reduction to essentials, his progressive stripping away of subsidiary elements, led him toward a severity of organization which recalls, deliberately one feels, the paintings of Herculaneum and Pompeii which had created such excitement in his generation. These paintings are characterized by broad planes of architecture which form flat and shallow platforms on which a few figures are placed in statuesque gravity [25]. They seem to conform to a vision rooted in relief sculpture, the same sculpture which David had studied and drawn so assiduously. In *Brutus* as in his *Oath of the Horatii* and *Socrates*, implied movements and sequence must move left and right, rather than on the diagonals of the baroque or the counter-curves of the rococo.

25. Herculaneum wall decoration. Engraving, 1762.

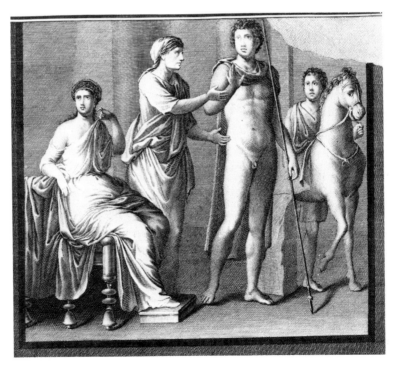

In the tradition of western painting, there are two artists to whom David should particularly be likened, Poussin and Giotto. Poussin was the obvious model for an artist like David. An erudite, worthy heir of the humanistic tradition, he had become the most revered figure in the French academic tradition. His mature style is a kind of square baroque, which matches the sculptured fullness of the Italian and Flemish styles without their curvilinear exuberance. The example he set David is best found in his deathbed scene of the *Testament of Eudamidas* (Copenhagen), which has the grave rhythms and noble simplicity that David admired.

Giotto should also be invoked, however, because there is a quality in David's style which looks back to early Italian art before Raphael.[23] His concept of pictorial order is based upon the juxtaposition of relatively autonomous forms more than upon the interlocked harmonies and counter-relations of Poussin. Poussin's figures are modeled with larger movements of light and shadow and they usually contain some elements that project forth in space in a commanding way. It is a great leap back to Giotto, admittedly, but perhaps a taste for him, aided by Roman wall painting and relief sculpture, would help account for David's distillation and purification of Poussin. Giotto and his school used a method of organization based on lateral apposition, and frequently exploited strong breaks between left and right sides of a composition as David did in *Brutus*. Of special significance is the possible origin in Giotto's era of this most unusual and controversial feature of *Brutus*, in which partly separate events are taking place on the left and on the right. In the acceptable conventions of their era, Giotto and his contemporaries often put two different events in one composition. The scenes are divided by a portion of a wall or a column, a device David used, and their figures accentuate the subdivision by facing away from the boundary column, a function performed by Brutus and by his swooning daughter, and also by the opposed chair backs. In contrast, when Poussin made a strong break between left and right sides in his *Death of Sapphira* (Louvre), he used a deep, piercing space-hole as a divider instead of a column, and had his groups face one another over the gap.

When David's painting was exhibited in 1789, and again in 1791, the critics drew attention to its separation into two parts, and to the placing of Brutus in shadow, as the marks of a new style 'virile, severe, terrifying'.[24] The consensus was distinctly in the artist's favor. The unusual placing of the protagonist in shadow was seen as an agent of emotional content which helped make Brutus 'sinister', 'terrible', which fortified the 'sad and lugubrious silence' and 'threw blackness into the soul of he who looks at it'. Brutus's execution of his own sons was so terrifying an act that he was a figure to be feared, and David made his contemporaries feel this, as well as his brooding isolation. Compared to the rococo style, the figure of Brutus seems almost like one of Michelangelo's damned, staring out of the smoky darks of the *Last Judgement*. The important element of awe is provided by the pose of the head and the gesture of the right arm, which hovers on a tone of command to silence. The head has snapped erect at the sounds of the mournful interruption and approximates the impact of the original Capitoline bronze [15] which gives visitors to Rome the feeling that behind it 'one can almost hear muffled sobs'.[25]

What David had done in the evolution of his conception was first to think of the execution scene, when Brutus had to display himself as consul, not as father. He then switched to the scene of private mourning, concentrating on Brutus's misery as father. As the composition evolved, the erect head and strong gesture became increasingly important, until in their final form they reassert the role of consul. It is as though the lower half of the body, with its writhing feet, its tortured folds of drapery and its insecure perch on the edge of the seat, embodies the father, while the upper half reveals the consul – that opposition of meditation and action incorporated in Michelangelo's *Isaiah* [23]. His erect head is given an upward nobility by making the funeral cloth behind spring directly from his neck, framing the head in an escutcheon of lighter tone. Placing the statue of Rome over the bodies of the sons, and Brutus next to both, is an obvious bit of symbolism, as is the implied contrast of Romulus and Remus on the pedestal relief, founders of Rome, with the two sons of the founder of the first Roman republic. More subtle is the echoing parallel of the left arms of Brutus and of his wife. His holds the letter to Tarquin listing his sons' names, a proof of treason which mocks the meaning of the piece of paper normally held by the 'seated philosophers' of Rome and by Michelangelo's Isaiah – their own writings. In contrast, the arm of Brutus's wife supports her living child, contrasting the mother's role with the consul's and with that of the statue-mother of Rome.

The separation of Brutus from his wife and daughters is the key to his character and to his position in history, and David decided to risk splitting his picture in two in order to make the point. Our eye leaps back and forth from the compacted side, with its masculine angularities shrouded in shadow, to the open side, with its feminine curves bathed in light. David uses the effort we must make to join the two sides in order to draw us into a dynamic process of comprehension. The main column and the symbolic empty chair form a barrier separating mother from her husband and dead sons, in contrast to the clinging proximity of her daughters. The daughters were not included in any prior treatment of the Brutus legend. David invented them to fortify the emotional appeal of the mother, to add variety of expression, and to accuse Brutus by their very existence of the deaths of their brothers.

The group of women has developed from the conception of the earliest drawings with as much subtlety as the Brutus figure. In the first drawing [2] there is merely a group of passive onlookers, retained in the final composition only in the weeping servant. In the next stages [4, 5, 7] the mother and daughters react by pulling away in horror. The daughter to the rear in these drawings seems to be helping her mother, instead of being dependent upon her, roles later to be reversed. The other daughter passes through a metamorphosis of fear until the motif of fainting is established. In its final form, the group shows a more complex reaction than in the initial one. The mother's horror has changed to supplication and she shelters her surviving children in her new role as a kind of Niobe. The upright daughter is turning away from the scene, as the swirl of her costume shows, but cannot take her eyes from the bodies. Her raised hands attempt to ward off the scene but are really a screen through which she sees. This is one instance of David's alertness to natural reactions, and is carried out by the meticulous position of the hands on the right side of the face, in view of the movement of the procession to that side of the girl's vision.

David's invention of this complicated play of emotions is perfectly in keeping with the appeal to sentiment we associate with art of the eighteenth century. The heart of the picture is a family torn asunder in the private misery brought on by the public act. The eighteenth-century 'soul' was seized by the picture; 'one despairs with the mother, one is moved to tears with the daughters, one groans over the fate of the sons, one shudders with the father'. Brutus had grown up in the king's household as a member of his family, surviving the murder of his parents; his fellow consul Collatinus was also a member of the royal family and his wife had been raped by the king's son; the brothers of Brutus's wife were among the chief plotters against the new republic. Something of the extent of these emotional disasters is found in the range of reactions in the picture, from the impassivity of the lictors and the stern brooding of Brutus, to the exclamatory despair of his wife, the fainting of one daughter, the transfixed horror of the other, and the submissive weeping of the old servant.

David contained the extraordinary emotional appeal of the scene by establishing a rigorous control over his elements, giving them a kind of rarefied, pressed-out clarity.[26] The women form a compact pyramid from which the limbs try to radiate out like a pinwheel. They are embraced by an oval of space established by the empty chair left of center and the other chair to the right. The striking still-

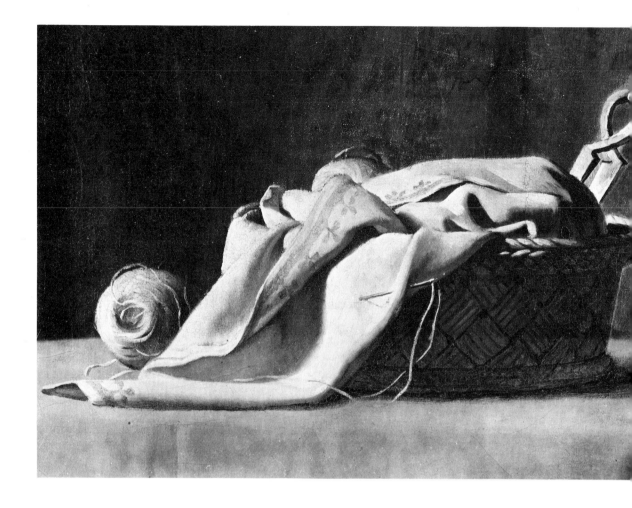

life [26] hardly seems like a bit of sewing hastily thrown aside, yet its unnaturalistic, Zurbaran-like starkness acts as a restraint upon the emotion-laden costumes nearby. Something of the same calming function is served by the table, whose feet, in contrast to the human feet nearby, support a cover whose solemn folds repeat the rhythm of the columns above. Intermediate between the columns and the figures are the descending showers of drapery folds which reiterate the fan shape formed by the three women together, and the small fan of blue cloth held by the weeping servant.

26, 27. *Brutus*, details.

The truth is that still-life elements, drapery and architecture are to David's era the nearest equivalent of abstract pattern in our own day [27]. Although the artist made them work as images, he felt free to manipulate them quite arbitrarily to the point that often their function as pure elements of pattern was uppermost in his mind. Teachers in art schools and Salon critics dealt with drapery and architectural settings as categories separate unto themselves. In *Brutus*, furniture and drapery have a more lively role than architecture, which establishes an easily read space, of a simplicity David thought appropriate to early Rome. His painted architecture is actually more like the work of contemporary neo-classical architects (Ledoux is the most famous) whose severe reform of prior modes had preceded his own reform of rococo painting.[27] Theatre design reflected the same changes on the eve of David's mature style, and the setting given Voltaire's *Irène* [6] predicts that of the painting.

Chiaroscuro, the play of light and shade, is as important as the arrestingly simple architecture in contributing unity to the subdivided composition. We have a sense of one powerful light flooding in from the upper left. It sweeps through the door to accompany the funeral procession, strikes the nearest column and the empty chair, and then merges with the other main shaft of light from the clerestory above to focus its full force on the despairing group of women. A subsidiary shaft of light seeks out the lower portion of Brutus, to make the more obvious the pool of darkness which he shares with the goddess, Rome. This pulsation of light and dark is one of the constant elements of the composition, and it has usually been overlooked in favor of the planar, sculptural modeling more readily associated with the neo-classical style. In this letter to Wicar (see Appendix) David stated his disdain for recipes of brushwork and handling 'as long as the lights are in their place', and from the *Oath of the Horatii* to the great *Marat* of 1793, there is a steady progression of dramatic quasi-baroque chiaroscuro.

His color and brushwork are also more painterly, more richly treated than is usually conceded. The strokes are full of life when studied closely, and move in the direction of the imaginary three-dimensional flow of the images. Draperies have a velvety thickness, rather than a hard surface, and flesh tones a translucent depth.

The color scheme of the picture is based upon an opposition of red and blue. The strongest red is the velvety tablecloth, which resonates against the intense blue of the weeping servant. A more diluted contrast is provided by the juxtaposition of Brutus's blue-gray garment to the bright red cushion. In the background above and in the left foreground the red component almost disappears, but it comes out strongly in the oranges and tans of furniture, floor and columns, and in the mother's garment. These somber red-browns, interspersed with patches of more intense red, evoke the blood in which the Brutus legend is steeped, from that of Lucretia's knife to the red on the severed neck of one of the sons, just visible at the rear of the procession.

The key to David's style in *Brutus* is in his own phrase in the Wicar letter, 'feeling and composition'. Although composition – the French word is *dessin*, which means draftsmanship and the concept of design all in one – is the servant of feeling, it was considered separately and somewhat artfully by the artist. *Dessin* had long been opposed to color and, to a certain extent, to *sentiment* because it was an intellectual component, associated with formal education in art schools, with perspective and geometry, and with the study of appropriate models, such as Poussin and the antique. Color was still largely outside the realm of rational, scientific knowledge, and was associated with the temporary and the instinctive. It was in any case subordinate to the guiding pattern of light and dark, the chief ally of feeling.

A compromise between the poles of strong feeling and rational control is the definition of David's style and its very mechanism. His instinct was for passion, and his career is marked by the emotional crises usually attributed to 'romantic' artists, including constant fights with his superiors, an attempted suicide, separation (and later reconciliation) with his wife, and a stormy public career followed by imprisonment in the Revolution. This instinct is manifested in the energetic, quasi-baroque style of his youth, and a strong penchant for the dramatic art of Caravaggio, Le Valentin and for Raphael's followers.[28] In the great pre-Revolutionary works and in *Marat*, David's passionate side is most readily felt in the strong chiaroscuro, and it is this side which is carried on in the next generation in the work of Baron Gros and Géricault. The other pole of David's art is the control he exercised over his passions, their constant disciplining by study of classical models, the admiration for 'primitive' styles which stressed planar apposition, the suppression of subsidiary details in favor of idealized, stripped forms. This side was subsequently developed by Ingres and Girodet.

Polarities of feeling and control are so thoroughly imbedded in David's art that they are inseparable from his choice of subject. The *Horatii* contrasts the feeling of women and the impending internecine murders with the sacrificial devotion to the cause of Rome. The *Death of Socrates* is another piece of individual heroism for an abstract cause, and of course *Brutus* is the most famous instance of human feelings being suppressed for the sake of the state.

The love of country which Brutus personified for Rome, David was shortly to demonstrate for France, as he finished his painting over the summer of 1789. It was two months after the Bastille had fallen that David sent to the Salon his *J. Brutus, first consul, has returned to his home after having condemned his two sons, who had joined the Tarquins and conspired against Roman liberty; lictors bring back the bodies so that they may be given burial.*

2. *Brutus and the Events of 1789*

In 1788 when David's *Brutus* was already underway, the national financial crisis had brought about great gains for the reform-minded aristocracy and for the middle class.[29] The convocation of the Estates General was announced, and in December the royal council doubled the representation of the Third Estate for the forthcoming sessions. The establishment of the delegations and the formulation of basic demands created a great outpouring of activity throughout France, an effervescence which was seconded by food riots as the May opening of the Estates approached. Sieyès's pamphlet of February, *What is the Third Estate?*, is one of the most famous of many assertions of middle-class rights against aristocratic privilege, and the reforms proposed by aristocratic liberals were tantamount to a demand for a constitutional monarchy. The tumultuous meetings of the Estates in May and June 1789 seemed to pit the aristocrats against the Third Estate with the king as the most important arbiter. After the oath of the Third (20 June) to remain in session as the National Assembly until the clergy and nobility joined them, the king ordered the other two to do so (27 June), and the first major stage of the middle-class assumption of power was reached.

Exasperated by severe food shortages, however, the bourgeoisie of Paris was dismayed by the dismissal on 12 July of the minister Necker, whose financial policies they regarded as essential, and this precipitated their fears of armed countermeasures which led to the assault on the Bastille two days later. The summary executions and sporadic riots which followed, fed by chronic food shortages, set the pattern for the rest of the summer, and led to the phenomenon of the Great Fear. This was an hysteria which spread over most of France, a compound of fears of aristocratic and foreign invasion, of famine and of near anarchy. Shops, residences of the wealthy, and sometimes whole villages were sacked, tax agents were manhandled, and wild rumors would exaggerate the number of violent deaths to fuel the mechanism all over again. These events, and the visible power of the new reformers in Versailles and Paris, encouraged a vast emigration of aristocrats. On 28 July the Assembly ordered a committee to study the alleged 'plots' of the aristocrats. It was under all this pressure that the delegates of the nobility at Versailles renounced their feudal privileges in the early hours of 5 August. That same night there began the deliberations leading to the Declaration of the Rights of Man and Citizen, whose provisional text, after constant discussion, was adopted on the 26th.

David was putting the finishing touches to his *Brutus* in this same month of August. Was he or was he not aware of the parallels with contemporary events that ultimately would give his picture a special fame? The gilded corruption of Tarquin's court could have been compared to the corruption of the French court that had brought on the great crisis. Tarquin's emasculation of the Roman senate could be likened to the suspension of the Estates General for more than a century and a half, and then to the recall and subsequent dismissal of the middle-class hero, Necker. Tarquin's exercise of tyrannical power could be paralleled by the *lettres de cachet* and the symbolic fortress of the Bastille. Once exiled, Tarquin and the Roman aristocrats plotted against the new government and conspired with Rome's traditional enemies. This could have seemed reborn in the wave of aristocratic emigration of the summer of 1789, and the fears of plots involving foreign powers.

On the other hand, Brutus's overthrow of tyranny and restoration of the senate could be recalled in the progressive renunciations of royal and aristocratic privileges and in the establishment of parliamentary power. Although few actually thought of deposing the king, the onrushing power of the liberals was evident to all, and the words 'liberty', 'freedom' and 'overthrow of tyranny' were heard on all sides, just as David was completing his painting of *Brutus*. The restitution of rule by law, assuming the proportions of national fervor, was a rebirth of the laws of Rome that Brutus had restored, and the concomitant qualities of frugality and moral rigor in the nation's leaders were echoes of his virtues. Brutus had even harangued the people (and angered Rome's aristocrats) in his rise to power, using mob enthusiasm as a political instrument – shades of Camille Desmoulins and the orators of 1789.[30] More particularly, David's painting could remind the Salon viewers of the summary execution of several 'enemies of the people' in that summer, and the final lesson of the picture, the sacrifice of the family to the good of the state, could be applied to king and government as a warning to clean house.

This potential for a political interpretation of David's *Brutus* is so evident that beginning with the Goncourt brothers of 1854,[31] historians attributed the picture's reception in the Salon to it, and usually credited David with a propagandistic intention. However, surprising though it may be, no account of David's picture in 1789 reveals awareness of the analogies with current events! On the contrary, David's own letter to Wicar in June 1789 (see Appendix) is full of longing for Italy and seems to imply that art is an escape from contemporary reality. And one of the most startling arguments against any contemporary gloss on his picture is found in the background of the Stockholm sketch [10]: above the funeral procession are the severed heads of the two sons, borne on lances. According to one of David's first biographers,[32] 'In the first composition, he had shown the heads separated from the bodies, and carried by the lictors. The frightful events of 1789 made him decide to hide them, as one sees them today.' The 'events' included of course the severed heads paraded about Paris in July: Delaunay and Flesselles after the fall of the Bastille, and Berthier and Foulon, considered responsible for food shortages, a week later. The suppression of the sons' heads for the final picture might indicate David's wish to avoid comparison with the present, and probably also indicates the exercise of elementary good taste.

Are we unable to resolve the conflicting possibilities of political and non-political interpretations? The answer will depend upon the retracing of an unusually exciting lesson in the use of circumstantial evidence.

We know enough of David's life to conclude that he was by nature a rebel against established authority. Of course he benefited from the state system, but so have many rebels, and in the two decades preceding 1789 he had constant disputes with the Academy's officials. Hardly any of the necessary steps upward were taken at the normal time in the customary manner; even his Salon entries were late and not always of the prescribed size. His students' letters of the mid-1780s expose the opposition he offered to the Academy and its methods, and to 'the wigs', his derisive term for his superiors. The events of 1789 simply enfranchised David's rebellious spirit. On 12 September, just as his *Brutus* was put on view, the Academy received a pamphlet, *Voeu des artistes*, which was a set of radical demands drawn up by art students, including David's. David must have entered into the discussion leading to the pamphlet – he could hardly have avoided them – and by mid-autumn he acknowledged himself publicly as the patron of the insurgents.[33]

What we know of David's friendships confirms the direction of his temperament. He frequented the liberal aristocracy and upper middle class who were soon to espouse the goals of the early phase of the Revolution: Lavoisier, the Duc d'Orléans ('Philippe d'Egalité' before long), Barnave, Lameth. David clearly shared the reformist spirit of 1788 and 1789, and it is likely that his wife did also. On 7 September, just before his *Brutus* was put on display, his wife joined in a singular demonstration of patriotic fervor. Twenty-one wives and daughters of artists, in white robes with sashes of the new tricolor, entered the Assembly at Versailles to offer their jewels as a contribution to the national debt, an event given extensive coverage in the press. It was emphasized that their inspiration came from the legend of Roman women sacrificing their jewels for the Republic, and also that 'The fine arts, by this sacrifice, have become associated with dawning Liberty. Accused of serving as ornaments to absolute power . . . Liberty is going to create for them a new society and new models.'[34]

The emulation of Roman virtue by the artists' wives and daughters bears the same relation to prior evocations of the theme, such as Brenet's *Piety and Generosity of Roman Women* in the Salon of 1785, as *Brutus* does to earlier and contemporary renderings of its theme. Revolutionary intention was not in the minds of artists who sought inspiration in classical art, but a moral intention was. The severity of David's neo-classical style was a moral and esthetic reform which was easily converted to political reform, because its target had been the elegant style of the rococo, associated with frivolity and absence of *virtue*, that cardinal word for the late eighteenth century. Brutus was *par excellence* the subject of virtue: avenger of woman's wrong, founder of liberty, restorer of law, inflexible magistrate capable of executing his own sons for the good of the state. From the middle of the century Brutus had been put forward by officials as a good choice of subject. Its future as a revolutionary theme would not be thought of when the state's virtue was not in question.[35] However, the peculiar adaptability of the story to liberal reform had tended to bring it forward most often in periods of challenge to established power. In the early Renaissance Brutus had had some prominence,[36] and it cannot be an accident that the maturing of Enlightenment thought on the eve of the French Revolution was accompanied by a Brutus syndrome. In French circles alone, Lethière and Wicar (David's student) embarked on Brutus compositions in 1788.

One of the most interesting of literary parallels is provided by the Italian playwright Vittorio Alfieri (1749–1803), who lived in France from 1785 to 1792. His plays on the early and the later Brutus were published in Paris early in 1789. *Bruto Primo* was dedicated 'Al chiarissimo e libero Uomo il Generale Washington', and *Bruto Secondo* 'Al Popolo Italiano Futuro'. The first Brutus is celebrated in a play bristling with calls to the new era, and the consul's inflexible will is cast into relief by the emotional appeal of his sons' love. The same appeal to sentiment that underlies David's painting is found at the very end, when Brutus sinks to his seat and to the chorus 'Yes Brutus is/The father and the God of Rome' gives the answer 'I am/The most unhappy man that ever lived.'[37] The 'sentiment' which readily distinguishes David and his period should not be used in order to deny appropriateness to the nascent Revolution.[38] Emotional appeal was a basic constituent of David's Revolutionary art. The great *Marat*, the lost *Lepeletier* and the *Bara* all rely on the pity roused in the spectator by contemplating (as in *Brutus*) the aftermath of an action, not its consummation.

The final piece of circumstantial evidence that points to the proto-revolutionary content of David's painting is his rejection of the Coriolanus theme, the one originally agreed upon in 1787. Why was Coriolanus abandoned in favor of Brutus? The actual reasons cannot be known, but some speculation is required, because the abandoned subject is a conspicuously 'monarchist' one, and Brutus is a 'republican' one. Coriolanus was a younger contemporary of Brutus, who gained favor as a hero fighting the exiled Tarquin and his allies. However, he sided with the wealthy citizens against the people on repeated occasions, and after his victory at Corioli (hence his name) became a leader of the aristocratic faction. The people banished him when he opposed measures to alleviate a famine, and he then went over to Rome's enemies. After successful attacks on Rome's territories, Coriolanus was about to assault Rome itself when his mother, wife and children pleaded with him to forsake his revenge. He did so, and was subsequently killed in a dispute with the Volscians.

From the vantage point of 1787, when there was hardly a hint of republican feeling, it seems clear that the themes of Coriolanus, Regulus and Brutus (as David was eventually to define the latter) have in common heroic acts of self-abnegation in which the pleas of women and children figure prominently.[39] Coriolanus showed a somewhat flawed heroism: he acceded to womanly appeals and thus suspended his revenge. In this sense, the women, more than

Coriolanus, are the heroes of Rome. In David's final choice, Brutus broods over the loss of his sons, and the emotional appeals of his wife and daughters are to no avail. This sacrifice of one's feelings to the state is even more notable than Regulus's act, because it sustained the newly founded republic. Compared with Coriolanus and Regulus, therefore, Brutus more clearly lends itself to a pro-republican interpretation. Besides, the severe food shortages and émigré plots of 1789 would have then recalled those of Coriolanus, and *he* could only have been found on the wrong side.

In the midst of the tumultuous events of the summer of 1789, there was issued the key document for the interpretation of David's *Brutus*. It is a letter of 10 August (see Appendix) from Cuvillier, of the royal fine arts office, to the painter Vien, president of the Academy, in response to one concerning the forthcoming Salon. Cuvillier was acting for the Comte d'Angiviller, the General Director of Fine Arts, with whom David had had a number of disputes over the years. Angiviller had been ordered into protective

28. *The Salon of 1789*, detail, 1789. C. de Wailly.

exile by Louis XVI, and had left Paris for Spain on 28 July. He remained away for six months. He was an intransigent royalist and the king probably feared he might become the target of popular action. At a time when compromise with the new spirit was essential, he was probably glad to be rid of an overly zealous servitor.[40] Cuvillier's letter was written, therefore, under the ominous cloud of Angiviller's exile.

After the first paragraph of the letter, which makes clear the importance of the Salon as a 'useful diversion' in troubled times, Cuvillier comes to his subject, the political screening of the pictures. He writes that Angiviller (who had left instructions behind) 'thinks that one could not exercise too much caution in the choice of subjects which will be exhibited, relative to the interpretations which might escape from an observer and which could be awakened by others. The theatre provides us each day with the most unexpected examples.' We shall see shortly that *Brutus* is one of the pictures he was worried about, but first we must examine a leading example of what he must have meant by untoward 'interpretations', namely the agitation surrounding M. J. Chénier's play *Charles IX*. It had been published in August 1788, but the royal censor forbade its presentation. Charles IX is shown as a weak king who allowed the Duc de Guise, Catherine de Medicis and others to carry out the infamous massacre of protestants on St Bartholomew's Day. The protestants, particularly Coligny, come out well in a play which clearly attacked court intriguers and the high clergy.[41]

Just before the fall of the Bastille, Chénier began demanding the presentation of his play in the National Theatre, but he was rebuffed by the royalist theatre committees. He embarked on a public campaign, seconded by prominent radicals like Brissot, Collot d'Herbois and Fabre d'Eglantine, and he wrote a pamphlet on liberty in the theatre that was widely noted in the press. Chénier's *De la liberté du Théâtre en France*, signed 15 June 1789, protested that the exposure of a tyrant two centuries after his death could hardly be cause for fear. On the contrary, an enlightened monarchy should welcome tragedies whose goals are 'moral and political' because they serve as instruments of public instruction for a 'free people', for an 'enlightened populace'. Chénier's pamphlet rings with such phrases, and concludes that if public interest is really followed, there will be a great revolution and 'to slavish arts there will succeed free arts; the theatre, for a long time effeminate and fawning, will henceforth be recalled to its proper goal, and will inspire in its productions only respect for law, love of liberty, hatred of fanaticism and execration of tyrants.'

Nine days after Cuvillier's letter, Brissot's journal *Le Patriote français*[42] printed a manifesto attacking royal censorship, and demanding Chénier's *Charles IX*, calling it a 'truly patriotic, truly political' play.

'This work inspires hatred of fanaticism, of despotism, of *Aristocracy* and of civil wars. The enemies of M. NECKER, this great minister, the Saviour of France, fear the resemblance that will inevitably be found between him and the Chancelier de L'hôpital, one of the characters in the play. The actors do not dare put it on at this moment. If you think that such a subject is worthy of your attention in these early days of French liberty, it is no longer court gentlemen who should give the orders. It is you.'

Under radical pressure, the play was put into rehearsal on 12 September, but in early October on the eve of its planned presentation, it was banned by the commune of Paris as likely to offend the king at a moment when reconciliation was in order. When it finally opened on 4 November it was a great success (among other reasons because of the first great triumph of David's friend Talma, in the role of Charles IX), and allusions to the present were common. The importance for David is that this history parallels that of *Brutus*: a liberal theme undertaken before the Revolution, then its radical potential enfranchised by the events of the summer of 1789.[43]

Other 'applications' of current events that Cuvillier feared in his letter could have arisen from portraits. In his third paragraph he

58

begins, 'The heading of portraits lets one more readily put oneself
on guard, because in general the sitters being known, one is in the
position of measuring public opinion and of not risking anything;
I imagine that concerning this, M. Lavoisier will be the first to
wish not to show his portrait.' Lavoisier and his wife, who had
studied art under David, had been painted the previous year by
David [29],[44] and this is the portrait in question. Why could it be

29. *Lavoisier and his Wife*,
1788. David.

subject to worrisome reaction? Lavoisier was a noble and a tax farmer, but he had long been greeted as a true reformer. The author of the Blois *cahier* of March 1789, he was the sponsor of proposals which favored constitutional restraints on royal power, and a member of the reformist '89 Club, along with Mirabeau, Brissot, Sieyès, Bailly and others. He was also, in his capacity as leading scientist, Commissioner for Gunpowder.

The suggested exclusion of Lavoisier's portrait was because of a violent incident that took place just four days before Cuvillier wrote to Vien. Lavoisier had ordered the removal from Paris of the stock of old, low grade powder, to make way for new. It was loaded on boats but seized by the people of the district. They feared Tarquin-like plots on all sides, and were convinced that the powder was being sent to aristocratic émigrés. On 6 August, Lavoisier was nearly hung by an angry mob, and only vindicated himself at the last moment. The clamor did not die down for several weeks, so Cuvillier had good reason to fear controversy if Lavoisier's portrait was exhibited.

Cuvillier next mentions Tollendal, whom he fears 'might renew the project of exhibiting this terrifying painting which it was so difficult to set aside in 1787; but at the same time, I am reassured [that Tollendal will see] the danger of furnishing more food to the fermentation.' *The Marquis de Lally-Tollendal Unveiling the Bust of his Father* [30] by J. B. C. Robin had been listed as No. 180 of the 1787 Salon but was excluded by the government as the exhibition opened. In 1789 Lally-Tollendal persisted (unlike Lavoisier who withdrew his portrait) and the painting, No. 157, appeared two rows below David's *Brutus* and next to his *Paris and Helen* [28].[45] It was a 'terrifying' picture because it evoked a singular instance of the ingratitude of kings. Lally-Tollendal's father had led the French forces to honorable defeat against the British in India, but he was made the scapegoat and charged with treason. After a long and highly controversial imprisonment in the Bastille, he was beheaded in 1766. The son, however, set about vindicating his father's honor,

30. *Lally-Tollendal*
Unveiling the Bust of his Father,
1787. J. B. C. Robin.

and in 1778 Louis XVI acknowledged a complete rehabilitation
and later praised Lally-Tollendal for his 'filial piety'. Robin's painting shows the son unveiling a bust of his father, while holding his
initial petition to the king, 'Sire, my father is not guilty'. It is an
ironic contrast to the nearby Brutus, who holds in his hand the
letter proving his sons' guilt.

It should not be thought from this that Lally-Tollendal was
opposed to the king in 1789. His portrait speaks more of pride of

self-accomplishment than of conflict with royal authority and, although favoring constitutional reforms, he was among the most prominent of the Assembly delegates for his energetic defense of the king. He was the author of the phrase for the king 'Restorer of French Liberty', decreed by the Assembly on 5 August, and he made constant calls to order in the face of that summer's agitation. He was steadily driven to the right and ultimately resigned his elected post in mid-October in protest over the leftward trend and the 'intimidation' of the king. Cuvillier's concern in August, a month after the fall of the Bastille, would none the less have been to eliminate any reflections upon royal justice.

Cuvillier, in the very next sentence after the phrase 'the danger of furnishing more food to the fermentation', finally comes to David. 'It is in this regard [that is, the 'fermentation'] that I am comforted, as much as I could be, by learning that M. David's painting is still far from finished; and, à propos this artist, I think as you, Monsieur, that his painting of *Paris and Helen* can be exhibited without remaining fears, by suppressing the owner's name.' The owner of *Paris and Helen* was none other than the king's brother, the Comte d'Artois, and his name was indeed dropped from the Salon catalogue.[46]

The painting that Cuvillier is pleased to find still unfinished is the *Brutus*.[47] David had informed Vien that it would be late, and in the Salon catalogue, No. 88, is the phrase 'it will only appear toward the end of the exhibition'.[48] Published Salon reviews noted that a number of pictures would arrive late due to the unusual circumstances of the summer, but in David's case such lateness was endemic. His major Salon pictures had often been delivered late, probably to inflate their impact.[49] By commenting on its unfinished state, Cuvillier implies a hope that perhaps it would never reach the public that year, but it was acknowledged a royal commission and so printed in the catalogue.[50]

Cuvillier's fears, one can guess, were not founded on the many precise parallels of the Brutus legend with current events, but on the general association with opposition to tyranny and still more on its evocation of bloody execution and funereal retribution in that period of turmoil.[51] In any case, events moved too quickly for Cuvillier's political screening. The Salon jury was deliberating while the Assembly (4 to 26 August) was elaborating the Declaration of the Rights of Man and Citizen. Vien, with Cuvillier's agreement, made the politic move of delivering in person the Salon catalogue to the Assembly just before opening day, 25 August.

Word of attempted censorship had meantime leaked out, and something of a specific political context was provided for the Salon. On 12 August, the new radical journal *l'Observateur* had reported in its lead article[52] that Angiviller had ordered Cuvillier to tell Vien

'to forbid the celebrated M. David, on behalf of the King who knows nothing about it, to exhibit a painting of his composition, representing the two sons of Brutus sacrificed by their father to the well-being of the Fatherland. The same Angiviller and Cuvillier, on behalf of the King, have also forbidden M. Barbier of the Academy of Painting to expose to the homages of the public his portrait of the Grenadier who raised the flag on the towers of the Bastille.'

The next day Cuvillier published a three-page reply to *l'Observateur*[53] in which he denied attempted censorship.

'I am certainly the friend, and perhaps a little the ally of the celebrated M. David: it is in light of these two relationships that he himself had his father-in-law notify me last week that his painting was not then and could not be finished. I know this work too well to refrain from pointing out that you are mistaken in your references to the subject of the painting, and that you deform it.

As for M. Barbier, I would have known nothing of his picture nor its subject, were it not for your paper.'

The rebuttal published by *l'Observateur*[54] claimed that on 11 August (the day after Cuvillier's letter to Vien), Vien had asked Madame David 'to warn her illustrious spouse that MM. d'Angiviller and Cuvillier have decided that he should not exhibit his *Brutus* in this year's Salon.' This article has the ring of truth about it and since all the dates interlock correctly, we can assume that upon receipt of Cuvillier's letter, Vien approached his former pupil through his wife. David refused to withdraw the picture and the mood of August did not permit Vien and Cuvillier to insist further. Vien instead inserted the notice of lateness in the catalogue he was then editing.[55]

When the Salon opened, J. J. P. Lebarbier's painting was on exhibition, No. 99: *Henri, called Dubois, soldier of the French Guard, who was the first to enter the Bastille*. Furthermore, there were other echoes of that signal event of the new era. Under No. 36, Hubert Robert showed a large painting of the Bastille being demolished [31], and on the same wall with *Brutus* [28] there hung Vestier's *The*

31. *Demolition of the Bastille*, 1789. H. Robert.

32. *Bastille Escapee*, 1789.
A. Vestier.

Bastille Escapee Henri Masers de Latude [32], No. 111. Latude had
several times escaped from the Bastille many years before, and in
his portrait he points in the background to the infamous prison
being demolished. He stands by his escape ladders, which were
exhibited in the courtyard of the Louvre during the Salon.[56]

The public mood on opening day is suggested by the *Révolutions
de Paris*.[57] After writing of the near-famine in Paris, it states,

'During this period in Paris, one paid a visit to the paintings exhibited in the Salon at the Louvre. The crowds were less considerable than in previous years. In effect, the allegories of love, portraits of courtesans, and flatteries of slaves interest us very little. Henceforth Brutus, pronouncing his sons' deaths, or Decius dying for his fatherland, that is what will please us and seduce us.' The writer had only glanced at the catalogue and assumed that David's subject was the traditional one of the execution, but the inference is clear. The irony is that Angiviller and Cuvillier would normally also have preferred heroic themes to fluffy subjects – a preference that was official policy – but the Revolution was placing a new construction on them.

The political potential of David's picture is certain, but the only references to it were those already mentioned, and no review of the Salon took up the issue. That more was not written is owing to the special circumstances of this Salon. David's picture was more than two weeks late, and therefore unavailable to the writers of the early reviews. By the time it was shown, daily events were so momentous that the press had little time for art and reviews were short and few. Besides, years of reticence born of government pressure could not be overturned instantly. Many reviewers, for fear of offending the king, would have kept their interpretations to themselves. The tradition was to comment on art as a world quite removed from contemporary events. For this Salon, for example, the portraits of Lally-Tollendal, the Bastille escapee Latude, and the Bastille hero Henri Dubois are given perfunctory remarks limited to the handling of paint and truth to life – but not *political* life, despite Latude's ladder in the courtyard.

junii Bruti imago

Nantes ce 28 avril 1790.

David

3. Voltaire, David, Brutus and the French Tarquin, 1790-93

David's participation in the Revolution, which eventually included public office and a whole range of activity, was at first limited to the immediate sphere of painting. Through the fall and winter of 1789–90 he continued his role among the dissident art students, and became their president. This was the origin of the moves against the Academy which he led, and which resulted in its abolition three years later. In the spring of 1790, his fame inspired the radical municipality of Nantes to commission a portrait of their mayor Kervegan. Although the painting was never completed, David was lionized by the citizenry of Nantes for an entire month.[58] At the home of an enlightened patron of the arts on 24 April, he was treated to an evening in his honor which resulted in a drawing of Brutus [33]:

'After having walked through the routes, alleys and paths of the picturesque garden, . . . David was greeted by the *Taking of the Bastille*, a new symphony . . . A little further on there rose up a temple of Liberty in front of which the artist removed his hat. After that, the way led to a rustic habitation where the banquet had been prepared. White statues, recalling the figures of David's paintings, decorated the banquet hall.

'During the meal, one spoke of a little of everything : . . . of *Charles IX*, of Joseph Chénier and of Talma, his principal interpreter, of Franklin's illness. There were drinks to Liberty and to the health of Mme David. But of course David was not forgotten, and those among the guests . . . who had had the good fortune of seeing *Brutus* in Paris rivalled one another in praising the painter and his work. David responded modestly, he objected. Then tired perhaps of the fanciful descriptions of his admirers and the questions of those who would have liked to have seen it, he took a pencil and indicated with a few lines the expression of his figure of Brutus.'

33. *Brutus*, 1790. David.

David's fame shone still more brightly as the year progressed. In June he took part in a commemoration of the Oath in the Tennis Court, and on 1 November, Mirabeau (on behalf of the absent Dubois-Crancé) proposed that his fellow Jacobins commission David to paint the subject.[59] Public subscription would pay for the huge picture (20 x 30 feet) and it would be offered to the National Assembly. This ambitious project was much discussed in the press, and ultimately decreed by the Assembly a year later.

In the liberalized Salon of 1791, David's large drawing of the Tennis Court Oath [34] was the principal attraction, and it consolidated his role as the semi-official painter of the Jacobins. He exhibited again his great pre-revolutionary pictures, the *Horatii*, *Socrates* and *Brutus*, and Charles Villette, Voltaire's principal champion, was inspired by them to state that David's 'burning patriotism directed his thoughts long before the Revolution'.[60] The patriotic interpretation of *Brutus* was so much taken for granted by now that the reviews wrote instead of the picture's emotional impact (see Appendix). This was David's last important Salon of the revolutionary decade. Thereafter he showed only an occasional portrait, and a few drawings or engravings after his works were exhibited. His two great paintings of the Jacobin period, the *Marat* and *Lepeletier*, were offered to the Convention, and exhibited in circumstances more exciting than any Salon. What happened was simply that his sphere of activity became more public and varied and, although he did many portraits, his efforts were increasingly tied to current events. His role in the public festivals was the dominant one, and after his election as deputy in September 1792, he served on a number of national and Jacobin committees. He was not the art 'dictator' he has sometimes been called, but we shall see that his activity as artistic advisor to the Jacobin revolution was a central one.

Voltaire's star, meanwhile, was fast rising in the early phase of the Revolution.[61] At his death in 1778 his body had been refused burial in Paris because of his attacks upon conventional religion.

34. *Oath in the Tennis Court*, 1790–91. David.

The controversy was reawakened in the Assembly in late September 1789,[62] when even the liberal clergy insisted on the need to expurgate a proposed edition of Voltaire's works. Voltaire's self-appointed heir Charles Villette and other radicals such as Saint-Just began an energetic defense of the philosopher which led to the celebratory presentations of his *Brutus* in November 1790, and then to the national homage of July 1791 – both involving David.

Already in October 1789, Saint-Just was proposing that Voltaire's remains be brought back to Paris for a national funeral,[63] and Villette carried on the campaign with great persistence. Voltaire's writings lent themselves readily to radical use, and some of the most common slogans of the Revolution were borrowed from his *Brutus* and his *Henriade*. The first linking of David with Voltaire is a case in point. The artist–authors of a Salon review,[64] when analyzing David's picture, cited the last line of *Brutus*: 'Rome is free, that suffices, let us give thanks to the gods', one of the slogans most often blazoned forth later. Early in 1790, one of the first 'Altars to the Fatherland' incorporated three citations from the *Henriade* and one from *Brutus*.[65] In July, the massive Altar to the first anniversary of

35. *Altar to the Fatherland*, 1790. Anonymous.

the fall of the Bastille [35] also bore citations from Voltaire. It had on its sides identical bas-reliefs of heraldically opposed groups of Romans taking an oath together, an inspiration from David's *Oath of the Horatii*.[66] Indeed the whole setting was inspired by antiquity, for the entrance of the Champ-de-Mars site was through a massive triumphal arch bearing imitation classical reliefs. The classical, rather than Christian *mise-en-scène*, was the one increasingly cited as appropriate to the Revolution, and by late 1792, in similar celebrations, the Christian portion retained for this early ceremony was abandoned. Perhaps the invocation of God still comforted the king in 1790 as he joined hundreds of thousands who faced the altar with its figured oath and its words from Voltaire's *Mahomet*, 'All mortals are equal; it is not birth / But virtue alone which makes the difference', and raised their hands to swear allegiance 'to the nation, to the law and to the king'.

Four months later, there came the presentation of Voltaire's *Brutus* by the National Theatre. By this time the politicization of the theatre had gone well beyond *Charles IX*, and an increasing number of plays celebrated revolutionary events. Collot d'Herbois's new play, *The Trial of Socrates*, opened at another theatre ten days before the Brutus revival, and it was studded with deliberate allusions to the present, including a kind of antique counterpart to the taking of the Bastille. The campaign for a reprise of *Brutus*, begun by Villette, was carried further by Mirabeau himself, who asked that it, Voltaire's *Death of Caesar*, and Chénier's *Charles IX*, be included in the ceremonies of 14 July 1790.[67] Opposition from the conservatives to the National Theatre was strong, for a new political meaning of the play was now obvious, although it had been produced off and on since 1730 (most recently in 1786) with no tokens of political opposition. The radicals, with Talma as their leading spokesman among the actors, eventually won out. While the play was in rehearsal, the *Chronique de Paris* warned the public in advance which lines to disapprove and which to applaud, and freely cited analogies with contemporaries. It stressed especially the oath of defiance to tyrants and traitors which Brutus and the senate take on the Altar of Mars at the beginning of the play and, using the phrase for the oath on the Altar of the Fatherland of 1790, asked if patriots 'will not find in this *serment fédératif* the expression of their own feelings?'

Voltaire's play begins with a dialogue between Tarquin's emissary Arons and Brutus that pits the concept of monarchy against that of a republic.[68] It seems clear to a modern observer that by opposing the extremes of a ruthless tyranny and a puritanical republic, Voltaire confessed his own preference for an enlightened monarchy, but in late 1790 his play would have seemed more radical. Brutus insists that Tarquin violated Rome's law and therefore lost his right to rule, a subordination of royalty to national law that was an accepted principle of the young Revolution, and the very basis two years later for the imprisonment and execution of Louis XVI. Throughout the play Brutus harangues his interlocutors with his hatred of tyranny and the necessity to defend republican liberty against the exiles.

> *If in the heart of Rome there be a traitor*
> *Who laments the king or who wishes a master,*
> *May he die a death full of tortures;*
>
> *Take care, Romans, no mercy to traitors:*
> *Were they our friends, our brothers, our children,*
> *Look only to their crimes and honor your oaths.*

Against the background of this inflexible opposition of liberty to tyranny, Voltaire places his central drama, the love of Brutus's son Titus for Tullie, Tarquin's daughter, and Brutus's love and trust in Titus. (Tiberinus, the other brother, is a weakling who is already won over to Tarquin, and he hardly figures in the play.) Titus is shown as the headstrong and victorious leader of Rome's battles, much disenchanted with the senate because it had not honored his victories with the consulate (he was too young). His love for Tullie,

36. *Mirabeau.* Anonymous.

74

and the promised position of heir presumptive, finally decides him to join the plotters. The conspiracy is uncovered before he can act, but he acknowledges that the momentary lapse was sufficient sin, and asks Brutus to condemn him as an example to Rome. Brutus, who sheds tears in his private interview with Titus, then assumes his public face and the play ends with his refusal to be consoled. Contrary to Livy and Plutarch, he does not witness the execution. When word is brought to him in the consul's home, he ends the play with 'Rome is free, that suffices, let us give thanks to the gods.'

Tension was high at the opening night of the reprise of *Brutus*, on 17 November 1790. Anticipating trouble, the city posted an ordinance forbidding canes or swords inside the theatre. The huge crowd, assembled long before the curtain rose, greeted Mirabeau with applause when he appeared in an upper box, and a delegation was sent up to urge him to accept an honored seat facing the stage. 'The French people', someone yelled, 'demands its Brutus!' There was again applause later when the audience pointedly applied to Mirabeau the words of Valerius to Brutus:

> *It is on you alone that our eyes are fixed:*
> *It is you who are the first to break our chains.*

This was one of Mirabeau's most important appearances in public outside the Assembly, and it is likely that he sought identification with Brutus. The recently rediscovered portrait of him [36], probably done after his premature death in April 1791, calls attention to the parallel. On his table sits a bust labeled Brutus, and on the wall behind him is a version of David's painting.[69]

The presentation of the play was extremely noisy. Constant interruptions extended the play to double its normal time. Royalists were still in good numbers and would applaud lines favoring their cause, but radicals would shout them down and cheer Brutus's defiance of tyranny. When Brutus sends Titus forth to defend the walls of Rome,

> *But I will see you victor, or with you die,*
> *Avenger of Rome, still free, without king.*

the audience, lest anyone doubt their trust in Louis XVI, cried repeatedly 'Vive le Roi!' and waved hats and handkerchiefs. This incident especially reveals the mood of November 1790. All the journals reported it as proof that Louis XVI was not likened to Tarquin, a fear that had been voiced earlier by conservatives as reason to oppose the play's revival. Affection for the king had waxed and waned since 1786, but the reformers wanted him as an ally against the diehard aristocrats. The theatre audience is referred to as 'children of Louis XVI' who expressed 'the liveliest homage of love to their Father' with their cries of 'Vive le Roi!' The good Father was by then under warning, however, and these cries were followed by thunderous shouts of 'Vive la nation! Vive la loi! Vive la liberté!'

At the end of *Brutus*, while waiting for the second play (a one-act comedy), the radicals in the audience asked for the bust of Voltaire. Houdon's famous sculpture was brought from its regular place nearby and put on the stage to cries of 'Vive Voltaire!' [37]. Because the stage floor was slanted, two Grenadiers volunteered to hold it for the rest of the evening. The bust was crowned with a laurel wreath by the actors, and the playwright Pieyre read an impromptu quatrain to the author:

> *The qualities of Brutus, better felt today,*
> *Find their place at last in the French theatre;*
> *You see them applauded by a new people;*
> *There lacks only Liberty for your success.*

The second presentation of the play two nights later was even more eventful. Before the curtain, the crowded theatre was treated to more impromptu verses, and one man stood on his seat to propose a public subscription for a marble bust of Brutus to be placed outside the theatre. When the curtain rose, the audience saw on one

37. *Voltaire Honored
at Revival of Brutus*, 1790.
Anonymous.

side the bust of Voltaire, and on the other, that of Brutus. The
painter of the *Oath of the Horatii* and *Brutus*, wrote the *Mercure*,

'M. David, whose patriotism is worthy of his genius, had had placed
on the stage a bust of Brutus which he had brought back from Rome.

A thousand thanks to him! What could be more august and more imposing than the sight of the first Founder of the Liberty of the Romans, and of the immortal genius who prepared our Liberty by his writings! In the illusion of enthusiasm, it seemed that these two great men were ready at any moment to come to life to receive the homage of the noble feelings they have aroused in the hearts of all.'

Between the flanking busts, the audience looked upon the Roman senate, led by Brutus and Valerius, assembled by the Altar of Mars, with the Temple of the Capitol to the rear, and part of the house of the consuls to the right. Before Vanhove, playing Brutus, could begin, a folder was tossed on the stage. Vanhove drew a sheet from it and read to loud acclaim,

> *O honored bust of Brutus, of a great man,*
> *Brought to Paris, you have not left Rome.*

The occasional scuffles of the first night were repeated and rival shouts interrupted the first act, but the radicals won the advantage and the play proceeded more normally thereafter. 'Never was illusion more complete', wrote the *Chronique*, 'the spectators were as so many Romans; they all thought of themselves as taking part in the action', and the *Mercure* spoke of the joy of those 'to whom the love of a Constitution still more favorable to Liberty than Rome's inspires already the feelings which ought to rise from their regeneration'.[70]

On the second night of the revival, the most remarkable event took place at the end of the play, with the stage still framed by the bust of Voltaire and David's copy of the Roman Brutus. The last acts take place in the consuls' palace, and the last scenes are the climax of the emotion of father versus consul. In the final interview with Titus, Brutus sobs as he forgives his son. He then refuses consolation after Titus is led away, and as Vanhove spoke the last line of the play, he slumped down in an antique chair just like David's, while in the background four lictors passed by bearing the body of Titus. 'Every Parisian', wrote Von Halem, 'knew David's painting;

each recognized right away the intention of thus honoring the artist in public, in front of the nation. It was like a national holiday, heightened by unanimous applause.' Subsequent editions of the play made this *tableau vivant* a regular epilogue with the new stage direction: 'Four lictors, bearing the body of Titus, cross the vestibule. Brutus sinks in an armchair. The curtain falls.'

A painting, having only one scene, cannot be too closely compared to a play, but David's is in essential harmony with Voltaire and with the treatment of the theme since its first major appearance in modern writing. Authors had freely invented new elements and usually disregarded Plutarch and Livy, partly to provide acceptable reasons for Brutus's condemnation of his sons.[71] It might seem that the actual scene of execution, avoided by Voltaire and by David, would have appealed more openly to the Revolution, but the admission of human feeling, the fact that Brutus had to conquer his emotions, was more in the nature of successful dramatic appeal.

David's intimacy with the theatre helps explain the congruity of his painting with the play. His extensive friendships among the actors, including the young Talma, would account for the loan of his bust of Brutus, and for the putting into action of his picture. Perhaps the staging of Voltaire's play in 1786 and earlier[72] had had some effect on David's choice of painted architecture. From contemporary prints [6] and other evidence we know that the consuls' house on stage showed Doric columns bearing a straight entablature, and one print (Moreau-le-Jeune's signed 1783) has a drapery attached to the columns as in the 1789 painting.[73]

David's pupil Delécluze later credited the *Brutus* picture with a revolution in costume and hair style, but we should doubtless link this with the Voltaire play also. Talma took the minor role of Proculus, but he had David help him design a simple cloth mantle and robe, and he had his hair cut short. Among bewigged actors clad in the rather ornate theatre version of 'classical' costume [38], his appearance caused a sensation. Madam Vestris remarked that he looked like an antique statue.[74] It was then that the French public

38. Voltaire's *Brutus*, illustration, 1826. A. Desenne.

began to emulate the new fashions of actors and artists, as so often happens. Wigs and powdered hair gave way to the more natural styles, graced by simple bands, of the men and women in the *Horatii* and *Brutus*, and women shed corsets and ornate dress for simple robes. These changes reflected the associations of the old style with the court (David had long referred to Academy elders as 'the wigs'), and the new not just with classical antiquity, but also with the virtues of simplicity, frugality and naturalness. Style is often the clothing of change and the ally of wilful morality.

The presentations of Voltaire's *Brutus* were quickly accepted as the triumph of 'democratic' theatre, amidst the rapidly growing power of the radical elements of the Revolution. The *Chronique de Paris* and the *Mercure* urged that *Brutus* be presented throughout France, since it had shown the power of the theatre to 'heat up the patriotic spirit more and more' (*Mercure*), and there were demands that free showings of the play be given to the common people as basic instruction.[75] 'Where is there at this time', wrote Von Halem, 'a play which like this one offers so many striking allusions to the present?' Until then, the royal theatre had a monopoly on Voltaire's and many others' plays, but this was eliminated in January 1791 by Assembly decree. The new freedom had been anticipated by 'patriotic' presentations of *Brutus* at Bordeaux, Nantes and Lille from late November onward, and it was performed thereafter with considerable regularity in the capital and in some of the provincial cities.[76]

Rome and the legend of Brutus became a staple of radical language in the wake of the Brutus revival. For example the journals of December 1790 were full of rumors of émigré aristocrats preparing to invade France. One of the most radical proposals was inspired by the stories of Brutus and Mucius Scaevola. A corps of one hundred 'tyrannicides' was to be formed to fight France's 'tarquinides'. In imitation of antiquity and of David's Horaces, they were 'to be armed by the very hand of the conscript father' at the Altar to the Fatherland,[77] a form later adopted for volunteer enrollees.

Rome's Pantheon was finally reborn a few months later.[78] Mirabeau, the leading spokesman of the Assembly, suddenly died, and on 4 April 1791 he was buried in the Panthéon, henceforth devoted by Assembly decree to the great men of modern France.

The national homage to Voltaire was decreed by the Assembly after Mirabeau's death, but before it could be carried out, the king was seized at Varennes (21 June 1791), while attempting to flee the country. Brought back to Paris a prisoner, he was immediately accused of being Tarquin. His bungled flight had led to the discovery of a proclamation he had intended to issue from abroad, which renounced his oaths to the new nation, and rallied émigrés and foreign allies against his country – shades of Tarquin among the Etruscans! The Cordeliers (Marat's club) put up a poster three days later which cited the lines from Voltaire's *Brutus*, with Louis and France substituted for Tarquin and Rome:

> *Think! On the field of Mars, that hallowed spot,*
> *Louis swore to be faithful and just . . .*
> *If in all France there be a traitor*
> *Who laments the king or who wishes a master,*
> *May he die a death full of tortures!*[79]

Contemporaries liked to speculate that on 11 July 1791, three weeks after his capture, the king must have observed the apotheosis of Voltaire from behind the closed curtains of his Louvre apartment. The night before, Voltaire's remains had reached Paris after a journey from Sellières on an ambitious but somewhat rickety chariot, described as 'half pastoral and half triumphal'.[80] It had rolled slowly through the countryside, greeted in each village by delegations and accompanied by a crowd. The sarcophagus was slung from four antique columns at the corners of the wagon, and was surmounted by a baldaquin. A rustic gallery of poplar, cypress, beech and elm surrounded it, sheltering a group who steadied the sarcophagus when it swayed too much. On the sides of the chariot were verses whose meaning would not be lost on the public after the capture at Varennes: 'If mankind has tyrants, it must depose them' and 'If man is created free, he must govern himself'.

The principal art work of the triumphal parade of 11 July 1791 was the second chariot, designed by the architect Célerier.[81] The

initial project [39] was somewhat simplified in the making, and
much of it was sculpted in plaster, suitably painted to resemble
stone or bronze. An approximate idea is given in contemporary
prints [40]. Bronze wheels supported a platform, embellished with
lateral draperies of blue velvet sprinkled with gold stars and
bordered in tricolor. The base of the sarcophagus had at its corners
four ornate candelabra in which incense burned. On the upper
corners were relief sculptures of winged genii in poses of mourning,
flanking the stirring lines from *Mahomet* and *Brutus*,

39. Chariot design for Apotheosis
of Voltaire, 1791. J. Célerier.

All mortals being equal, it is not birth,
It is virtue alone which creates differences.

. . . but he must especially love the laws;
He must be their slave and bear all their weight.
Whoever violates them cannot love his country.

40. *Voltaire's Remains Transported to the Panthéon, 1791.*

An antique bed rested on the decorated lid of the coffin, and bore the image of a recumbent Voltaire. He was swathed in drapery with his upper chest exposed (as David was later to exhibit the bodies of

Marat and Lepeletier), and by his side hung a broken lyre and a laurel wreath. At his head, as though just alighted, was a figure of winged Immortality, holding over the writer a crown of stars. To complete what was intended as an imitation of the antique, the chariot was pulled by twelve white horses, unaccoutered except for a simple harness and tricolor cloth, and led by men dressed in antique costume.[82]

With the chariot at its heart, the vast cortège set out from the demolished Bastille in mid-afternoon, delayed by a rain which returned periodically to soak the participants. Several tens of thousands formed the long line. They were organized by groups, which included the Assembly delegates, the National Guard, groups of musicians, students, and representatives of the professions. Academy models in Roman costume carried on an antique litter a plaster replica Houdon had supplied of his famous seated Voltaire. The Kehl edition of Voltaire's works was borne along in a gilded cabinet, and many groups carried banners with citations from his writings, especially from *Brutus*. Art students marched with imitation Roman standards, lyres and crowns, the women dressed in white robes with crowns of roses on their heads. Some carried busts or medallions of modern heroes, of whom Voltaire, Rousseau, Franklin and Mirabeau were the most prominent. Among several groups of musicians was one whose instruments and costumes were inspired by the sculptures of Trajan's column and other antique sources (the *tubacorva* was agreed to be the greatest success).

The march went along the Boulevard St-Antoine to the Opera, where it stopped for the first of several 'stations'. A bust of Voltaire, placed on an antique altar, was crowned by singers who recited words from his *Samson*. The cortège then took a long route to the quai of the Tuileries, where it passed under the windows of the king. The *Chronique de Paris* remarked – and the remark is typical – that contemporaries 'were struck by the great contrast presented by the philosopher entering in triumph within the walls of Paris and receiving the honors of an Apotheosis, and the fugitive Louis XVI, brought back and retained captive in his own palace by his justly indignant sovereign [the people].'

The procession crossed the bridge from the Louvre to the home of Charles Villette, where Voltaire had died. Its façade was decorated and in front, facing temporary grandstands, was a special amphitheatre. Its dome, surmounted by a crown, was made of green branches and leaves, and it was flanked by poplar trees. It sheltered fifty young women dressed in white antique robes with blue sashes and crowns of red roses. Mme Villette stood between the two daughters of Calas, the protestant martyr whom Voltaire had vindicated. She was dressed in mourning, with a sash [41] on which an

41. Sash commemorating Voltaire's Apotheosis, 1791.

apotheosis of Voltaire was embroidered. When Houdon's statue of Voltaire reached the amphitheatre, Mme Villette, weeping, carried her infant daughter to it, rested her head on the statue's breast for a time, and placed a civic crown on its head.

Meanwhile, Célerier's imposing chariot remained on the Pont Royal 'where it presented a most imposing aspect. Before it arrived in front of the house, a lugubrious music expressed pain and mourning, but soon the sadness of funereal regrets gave way to the joy of immortality and to the verses of an ode by M. Chénier, set to music by M. Gossec, executed in part on antique instruments copied from Trajan's column . . .'[83] Among the verses of the Chénier–Gossec hymn to Voltaire, one reads:

> *Your tragic pen has brought to life*
> *The ancient virtues of the Tiber's demigods,*
> *And France has voiced the need to be free*
> *In the proud accents of the two Brutuses.*

The next major station was the National Theatre on the Place de l'Odéon, embellished with a large painting of two genii flanking a bust of Voltaire, and with various signs, titles of Voltaire's plays, garlands and banners. The Houdon replica arrived to the sound of the opera *Samson* 'whose words', wrote the *Chronique*, 'seem to have been written since the Revolution':

> *People, rise up, break your chains!*

Several actors stepped through the curtains of a 'sanctuary of light' to make offerings to Voltaire. 'Brutus' gave a bundle of laurel, 'Orosmane' a flask of Arabic perfume, and 'Nanine' a bouquet of roses. It was by then dark and raining, so the procession hurried to an abbreviated ceremony in the Panthéon. About midnight, in the building originally planned for Ste Geneviève, Voltaire's sarcophagus was placed on an altar base of granite. It was the climax of a remarkable day devoted, as the *Chronique* wrote, to 'the triumph of reason, the defeat of fanaticism, the sacred love of Fatherland and the resolution to sacrifice everything to Liberty.'[84]

The contrast between Voltaire's posthumous fame and the captive Louis XVI grew over the next year, and the dramatist's play was increasingly used to judge the king's actions. It was the revival of *Brutus* in November 1790, augmented by David's painting, which had provoked the first actual comparisons between France and Brutus's Rome. Voltaire's play had stressed that sovereign power rested in the nation's laws to which even the rulers must swear allegiance. The French of 1790 tended to agree with Voltaire's thesis, which wished to oppose to the self-seeking aristocrats a strong government faithful to the law. The potential for a radical use of the Brutus legend was not at that time in a comparison of the king with Tarquin, but in the subordination of royal autonomy to national law. The repeated oaths Louis was required to take to the succession of new laws bound him increasingly to this concept, so that if he violated them, he would be guilty of Tarquin's crime.[85]

Seven months after the revival of *Brutus* the king had made his abortive attempt to flee the country. He none the less survived because he was needed as an instrument of the revolutionary coalitions. Then, with the outbreak of war in the spring of 1792, tensions built up to a new pitch, and the disclosure of Marie-Antoinette's correspondence with the enemy seemed to confirm the fear that Tarquin and his family were in the bosom of the nation.

On 15 April 1792, David directed a public Festival of Liberty in honor of the Swiss guards of Châteauvieux (punished the year before for refusing an order now regarded as counter-revolutionary). David, M. J. Chénier and others signed a public letter calling attention to the festival which was to honor 'resistance to despotism' and 'heroic disobedience'.[86] The principal artifact in the parade was a Chariot of Liberty [42] designed by David. It was

'mounted on the same wheels which served the chariot for Voltaire's apotheosis. This little fact has its value: we should not forget that it is philosophy which has brought us liberty.

42. *Festival of Liberty, 1792*, detail. After J. L. Prieur.

'The chariot, modelled on the antique, offers an imposing mass. On one of its sides, the gifted painter of the Revolution, M. David, has outlined the historic act of the elder Brutus, condemning to death his sons, victorious but disobedient to the law. The other lateral part represents William Tell, aiming a javelin . . .'[87]

The reliefs on the chariot were a deliberate threat to the royal family and the aristocrats. Had not the David–Chénier letter echoed the severity of Brutus by proclaiming that the new France 'knows how to recompense the supporters of liberty, just as she knows how to strike the conspirators even on the steps of the throne'? This is why David chose Brutus condemning his sons for the relief. The act of judgment suited the purpose better than the scene of private mourning which he had painted in 1789.

In the first week of June, Prudhomme's *Révolutions de Paris* gave over its issue to a long restatement of the Brutus story, beginning with a remarkable set of juxtapositions and the precocious use of the word 'republic':

'One sees that in all periods, in all places, revolutionary overthrows of empires are nearly the same. The Roman republic thought it would be destroyed in its infancy. From its origin, enemies have wanted to destroy the French republic. A party in favor of Tarquin was formed in Rome; there is one formed in Paris favoring Louis XVI. Young people, the first of the city, raised at the court and nourished in license and pleasure, undertook the reestablishment of Tarquin. The young nobility of France . . . have undertaken the reestablishment of Louis XVI.'

Louis XVI, he said ominously, 'is the Tarquin of our day'.

In July and August the fears of conspiracy from within and the actual war on the borders further excited the nation. The savage battle at the Tuileries palace on 10 August [43] led to near anarchy, and the king was finally deposed. In September the Assembly voted to disband in favor of a constitutional Convention, and the Republic was proclaimed on 22 September.

43. *Storming of the Tuileries,*
10 August 1792.
J. Duplessis-Bertaux.

Throughout this period the particular nature of Brutus's republic gave it special relevance. His image was literally reborn to watch over the foundling republic. On 22 August the session of the Jacobin Society was devoted to demands that the king and his family be judged for their crimes.[88] Terrasson ended a speech with the cry,

'"Judge Louis XVI, judge Marie-Antoinette, it is the will of the sovereign people."

'A bust of Brutus is brought into the room and is received in the midst of universal applause.

'M. Manuel: "It is here that the fall of the kings, the fall of Louis the Last was prepared, and it is here that should rest the image of the one who was the first to wish to purge the earth of kings. Gentle-

men, here is Brutus, who will remind you at every turn that in order
to be a citizen, it is always necessary to be ready to sacrifice everything, even your children, to the welfare of your country . . . We
must each swear the oath, and I will be the first, that at whatever
post we find ourselves, all our efforts will be directed towards this
important goal, to purge the earth of the pestilence of royalty." All
hands are raised at the same moment, and the oath is pronounced
with energy.'

The bust was the work of the artist Lenain, who offered its repro-
duction at modest cost. The proposal was passed that it be adopted
officially by the Jacobin Society for each of its member groups, with
the legend 'The Mother Society has taken Brutus as its patron'.

In the National Assembly itself, where the Paris commune and
the Jacobins were now so powerful, the sculptor Joseph Boiston
appeared on 1 September and offered a marble bust of Brutus [44].[89]
He had just returned from Rome where he had executed the bust,
a facsimile of the same Capitoline bronze that had inspired David's
painted *Brutus* and a copy of which David had placed on the stage
for Voltaire's play. Amidst thunderous applause, the bust of this
'hero of liberty' was accepted, and a decree passed that it be kept in
the national meeting place.

That autumn and winter *Brutus* looked out upon the new Convention as it debated the fate of Louis XVI. Some crucial victories
of the revolutionary armies added a tone of wild enthusiasm and
pride to the mood of Paris, but fears of counter-revolutionary
conspiracies were hardly allayed. On the contrary, from early
November onward, the Convention – in which David now sat as a
deputy from Paris – was treated to reports of the secret papers of
the king found at Versailles, which proved his steady correspondence with foreign and émigré royalists, and with domestic 'moderates'. These latter included some leading Girondists, and their
exposure in early January gave the final say to the radicals who had
been demanding the king's execution.

44. *Brutus*, 1792. J. Boiston.

There was no legal precedent for such an act, of course, and so there occurred a remarkable phenomenon: the text for the judgment, the 'precedent', was the Brutus story. Invoked countless times by the orators, it had no rival. (Since Cromwell was regarded as a self-serving usurper, the execution of Charles I was not treated as a proper analogy.) It was upon early Roman history that Saint-Just drew on 7 November[90] when he adduced proof of Louis's crimes, crimes that had led to the spilling of blood 'one might say, up to your feet, even up to this image of *Brutus*' (Boiston's bust). Guilt proven, judgment also comes from Rome. 'There was nothing in Numa's laws by which to judge Tarquin', because a monarchy will not make provision for its own demise – and the Convention has the authority because it *is* the people. On 3 December, Robespierre is one of several who repeat these arguments: 'In what republic was the need to punish the tyrant subjected to litigation? Was Tarquin brought to trial?' The same day, Camille Desmoulins climaxed a long speech with the inevitable parallel:

'And have we anything else to do right now than what Brutus did when the people gave him his two sons to judge . . . ? He had them come before his tribunal, as you ought to make Louis come before yours. He produced proof of their conspiracy, as you ought to produce for Louis XVI this multitude of overwhelming proofs of his plots. . . . and it only remains for you to prove, as Brutus did to the Roman people, that you are worthy of founding the Republic and its constitution . . . by pronouncing the same judgment: *I, lictor; deliga ad palum.*'

The day following this speech, the Convention decreed that death should be the punishment of 'whoever proposes to reestablish kings or royalty', in direct emulation of Voltaire's *Brutus*, where such an oath is sworn in the first act. The most thorough-going of many invocations of Brutus was that of the artist Sergent who, like David, was a deputy. He urged execution as the logical application of Brutus's judgment to France's dilemma.[91]

The king was found guilty by a large majority, and the debates on exile, imprisonment or death were resolved by the vote of 361 to 360 for execution. The artists David and Sergent voted with the majority, and so did Philipe d'Egalité, formerly called the Duc d'Orléans.

The erstwhile 'father of the people', having become France's defeated Tarquin, the sentence was carried out before the eyes of the people on 21 January 1793. There later appeared on the streets an anonymous broadside[92] showing a republican next to the tree of royalty he has chopped down, and below are six lines from Voltaire's *Brutus* with appropriate changes, beginning 'If in the heart of France there be a traitor . . .'

Jeudy 24 Janvier 1793. le Corps du Martyr de la Liberté , sorti de la maison de son frere et couvert à demié sur
son lit de mort, fut exposé sur le piédéstal de la Statue de Louis XIV. Place des Piques ci devant Place de Vendome .

45. *Exposition of Lepeletier's Body*, 1793. Anonymous.

4. David, Brutus and Martyrs to Liberty, 1793-4

Now that the king was gone, the unity of the nation had to be emphasized, and on 27 January a festival was held on the Place du Carrousel, within the arms of the Louvre. An oak 'tree of brotherhood' was planted, and 'among the emblems that one usually sees in our patriotic festivals, one noticed in this one the bust of Brutus, the enemy of tyrants. The oath of unity, and the one to uphold liberty, equality, the indivisibility of the Republic at the peril of one's life, were renewed with enthusiasm.'[93]

The need for rallying the nation around new symbols was served especially by a notable martyrdom, a murder which seemed to prove that royalist plots were indeed to be feared and was therefore an act which vindicated the regicide. The day before the beheading of the king, Michel Lepeletier de Saint-Fargeau, for having voted with the majority, was stabbed to death by a member of the former royal guard. David was asked to arrange for 24 January a public exhibition of the body of this first major 'martyr to liberty'. Around the pedestal of the destroyed statue of Louis XIV in the Place de Vendôme he built a raised base with lateral steps [45]. Candelabra and tripods, imitating the antique, sent up clouds of perfume. Above, David had Lepeletier's body placed on an antique bed, the upper body exposed to show the wound, the assassin's sword hanging from the bed, and the victim's clothing mounted nearby on a beribboned standard. At the height of the ceremony members of the Convention stood on the steps while their president crowned the body with the wreath of immortality.

The whole presentation with its antique trappings was intended to evoke Rome. David had once copied a Roman lamentation scene in which the warrior's body, with chest and arm exposed, was placed on a bed.[94] None the less, the wound in Lepeletier's side was a witness to the first and greatest Christian martyr, and the position of the body is that of any number of tomb sculptures of earlier times, and of recumbent Christ figures. Still another evocation is the sculpture of the half-nude Voltaire which surmounted the chariot in his apotheosis. What David had done was to fuse elements of the secular and religious past, supplanting them as the Revolution had supplanted the old regime.

A month later, David asked the Convention to place the bust of Lepeletier by Fleuriot, being offered to the nation, next to that of Brutus.[95] From all sides there rained down on the Convention copies of addresses and letters honoring Lepeletier.

'That Brutus, called upon to judge one of his own accused of treason against liberty, forgot blood ties and condemned him, that is an act of virtue! Would Lepeletier be less virtuous in condemning the head of this superb nobility of which he had been a member himself? But there is this difference between Brutus and Lepeletier: the former did not have to face the challenge of confirming his sentence in face of the raised arm of a menacing assassin.'[96]

David's homage to Lepeletier was his painting offered to the Convention on 29 March 1793. It was later destroyed by the martyr's family, and is known only by a mutilated engraving and a few drawings after it by other artists. It showed Lepeletier in the pose of the exposed body in the Vendôme, the upper body nude, the head tipped forward and one bent arm uncovered. In his short speech to the Convention[97] when presenting the picture, David documented his appeal to feeling:

'Citizens, the firmament which spreads its gift among all its children wills it that I express my soul and my thought by the organ of painting . . . and I will have fulfilled my task if one day I make an old father, surrounded by his numerous family, say "Come, my children, come see the representative who was the first to die in order to give you liberty . . ." '

David was by now one of the more prominent members of the Convention. He had been made a member of the powerful Committee of Public Instruction in October 1792, and also a member of the Art Commission. The vitiated Academy tried to court his favor in April 1793 with an invitation to teach, but his entire reply consisted of the chilling phrase, 'I was formerly of the Academy'. All official art and public projects were now initiated by the Convention or by the city of Paris, and David was often on the supervising committee.

David had a modest advisory role in the designing of the new meeting place of the Convention. In the last month of the old Assembly, September 1792, it was decreed that the large theatre in the Tuileries palace should be made over as the legislative hall.[98] David served on a committee of four which steered the rebuilding along its uneven path. The Convention inaugurated its new hall on 10 May 1793, in the conviction that its classical style was a fitting home for the reborn Roman republic. Above the doors of the entry room were the attributes of Liberty and Equality and medallions of Brutus and Solon in bronzed stucco. One came next to the Liberty Room, painted in imitation stone and housing a colossal bronzed statue of a seated Liberty. In the large legislative hall itself, the deputies' seats formed a curve facing the president's imitation consular chair and the rostrum. Above on the speakers' side [46] were enormous painted statues of Demosthenes, Lycurgus, Solon and Plato, and opposite them, in a kind of antiphonal Plutarch, were Camillus, Publicola, Brutus and Cincinnatus.[99]

It was Brutus who gave particular emphasis to the setting of a *senatus romanus*. Speakers faced his painted image on the wall opposite, and his sculptured bust [44, 46] was placed in front of the rostrum. Orators sometimes swore 'on the head of Brutus' and as frequently pointed to him when invoking the principles of just law.

46. *Ferraud Assassinated, 1795*, detail. J. Duplessis-Bertaux.

The most chilling reference was that of the Duc de Chartres, the father of Philippe d'Égalité. When the son was accused of being a Girondist traitor, the father replied 'If my son is one, I see from here the image of Brutus'.[100]

An additional hero of liberty was provided to the Revolution in the summer of 1793. David was finishing his month as president of the powerful Jacobin Society when news was brought on 13 July of the assassination of Marat. The 'friend of the people' was an ally of the Jacobins and only the day before, David had visited him on their behalf. He had found Marat writing on a makeshift wooden desk next to the tub in which he was bathing his diseased skin. David proposed to display the body that way for public funeral, but its condition required a hasty ceremony and burial, and it was exhibited briefly on a raised pallet with the upper chest exposed and the bathtub nearby. The painting he now began would present Marat in his tub as David had wished [49].

Marat's death came at a critical moment. The Mountain had executed some of the leading Girondists the previous month, and stood in need of a hero-martyr to vindicate them. Marat could serve that function, as Lepeletier had at the time of the king's assassination. The Convention accepted a bust of the hero by Beauvallet, and decided to keep it on display next to Brutus, Lepeletier and the military hero Dampierre, killed in battle in May.[101] The latter was not there just as a martyr to liberty, but as a call to military action. The revolutionary army was suffering severe reverses in the late spring and early summer, and the situation was worsening. Internal dissension was also at a critical stage. The city of Lyon had been taken over by counter-revolutionaries and the Vendée was in arms. A veritable national mobilization in August created an explosive atmosphere in which heroes and symbols were desperately needed. The cults of Marat, Lepeletier and Chalier (killed at Lyon in July) began to spread rapidly, to reach their climax in early autumn.[102]

Meantime David was put in charge of the festival of Republican Reunion to commemorate the events of 10 August 1792. His elaborate program, published by the Convention in July,[103] drew upon past festivals and foretold the greatest of them all, the festival of the Supreme Being of June 1794. Among the ceremonial figures was a large fountain of Regenerated Nature on the site of the Bastille. From its breasts water came forth to be drunk one by one by the delegates from the various departements. The cup they used had been brought back from Rome by a sculptor who was among the first to rename himself Brutus: Brutus Dudevant.

The commemorative medal which David designed for the Reunion festival of 1793 also represented 'our common mother, Nature, pressing from her fecund breasts the pure and salutary liquor of regeneration',[104] and in proposing it he recalled those oaths to unity and the nation which had been predicted by his own *Oath of the Horatii*, and repeated at the unity festival, 'the sublime spectacle of a nation of brothers embracing one another and swearing in unison, under the celestial vault, to live republicans and to die republicans'. After the oath, the eighty-six delegates of the nation gave to the president of the Convention the separate branches each had carried in the festival, and he rejoined them with tricolor ribbons to form the fasces of the Republic. Some reflection of these rites is found in *Liberty and Equality united by Nature* [47], an undated engraving of Ruotte which probably celebrates the summer festival of 1793. Busts of Brutus and Mucius Scaevola surmount fasces and crowns of immortality. Nature in the form of Diana of Ephesus presses her breasts of regeneration, while Equality with her scales and Liberty with her club of vigilance join hands over the flame of the Fatherland. It is as good a lesson as any of the frequency with which moments of great crisis are embodied in images of steely calmness.

The central role of art in the crisis of 1793 continued and grew, as the fortunes of the revolutionary army began to improve in September. There had been a levy of the entire male population in late August, and various groups, especially the radical 'Sections' in Paris, vied with one another in sending volunteers to the front. The attributes of church and royalty, being removed from public eyes,

47. *Liberty and Equality
united by Nature,*
c. 1793. L. C. Ruotte.

48 (*right*). Lepeletier,
Marat, Chalier, *Martyrs to Liberty,*
c. 1793. Anonymous.

were melted down for arms, a symbolic and a practical metamorphosis. The occasional military successes of early autumn rewarded
the fervor of the Sections, which began to develop ever more elaborate formalities to honor their volunteers. These centred about the
martyrs to liberty: Marat, Lepeletier, Chalier . . . and Brutus.[105]

On 12 September 1793, the Section de Molière et Lafontaine
took the new name of the Section de Brutus, and on the 15th held a

ceremony with speeches honoring Marat and Lepeletier. The Section du Panthéon had its similar rites on 22 September, and installed busts of Marat, Lepeletier and Brutus. This triumvirate (with the frequent addition of Chalier) entered into the ceremonies of most of the Sections. On 6 October, the combined Sections of the Halle-au-bled and William Tell began their solemnities in front of an outdoor platform on which were the busts of Marat, Lepeletier and Brutus, and the Declaration of the Rights of Man framed in stones from the Bastille. Trees of liberty were planted, then the three busts and the Declaration were placed 'on draped litters, and carried by citizens dressed in Roman costume' to the Place des Victoires.[106] There the busts were set on a raised platform [compare 48], and speeches given. A few days later Palloy, the Bastille cultist, told the two combined Sections that he would subsidize the replacing of the obelisk in the Place des Victoires by the Declaration, to be surrounded by four columns made of Bastille stone. These would be capped by busts of Brutus, William Tell, Marat and Lepeletier.

In the midst of the constant turmoil of the early autumn, David found time to finish his painting of Marat [49].[107] It was revealed to the public in an extraordinary solemnization on 16 October. The Louvre Section to which David belonged inaugurated busts of Marat and Lepeletier that day in a long funereal holiday. The line of march led to the old courtyard of the Louvre, where David's paintings of the two martyrs had been placed side by side, each on a sarcophagus and surmounted by a chapel whose description is lacking, but which must have been of rustic branches with tricolor drapery. Such a setting would have resembled a Christian chapel, all the more so because the two heroes have the poses frequently given to Christian dead.[108] They would have had striking emotional force, as David's Section sang funeral hymns in front of them and repeated oaths to die for the nation. Although it was perhaps an accidental association, Marie-Antoinette had been guillotined a few hours earlier that same day.

MARTIRS DE LA LIBERTE

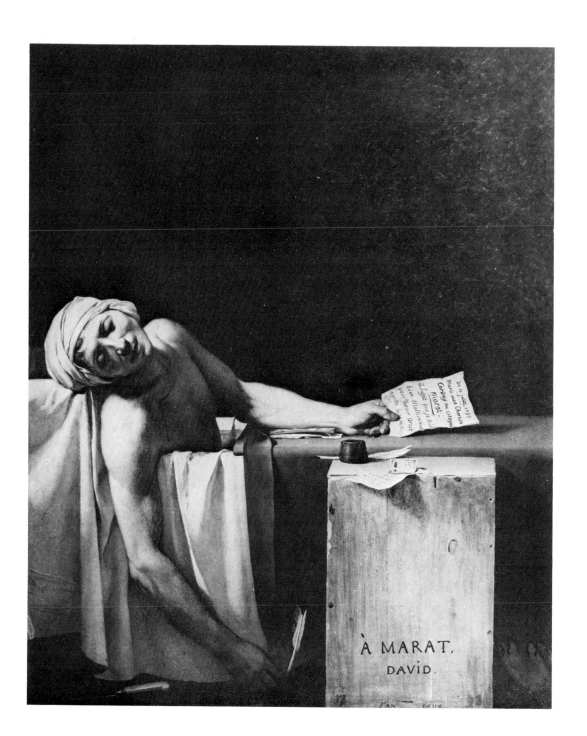

From the autumn of 1793 until the fall of Robespierre and the Jacobins, the images of Marat, of Lepeletier and of Brutus were present in public chambers, in streets and in homes. Marat tended to dominate the contemporary heroes, and as for Brutus, he had no rivals among classical figures. It was his role as judge of men's actions which made him so omnipresent. Sometimes he was paired with Mucius Scaevola, who stood for the virtues of the young militant activist, but this only fortified Brutus's position as magis-

49 (*left*). *Marat*, 1793. David.

50. *Royalty Annihilated, c.* 1794. Anonymous broadside.

LA ROYAUTE ANEANTIE
PAR LES SANS-CULOTTES DU 10.

UNITÉ, INDIVISILITÉ DE LA RÉPUBLIQUE,

FRATERNITÉ, OU LA MORT.

Je renverse tout, je fauche tout. Je suis fils d'un Sans-Culotte : je porte en mon cœur la Liberté, l'Egalité gravées, et la haine des Rois.
La France a mes soins, mon cœur ne connoit qu'elle. Père, Fils, j'immolerois tout ce que j'ai de plus cher au salut de ma patrie ; et je dirois comme Brutus, après ce sacrifice :
— La France est *libre, il suffit, rendons graces aux Dieux.*

A PARIS, chez Avon, rue de Bièvre, N°. 47.

J. BRUTUS.

Dieux! donnez nous la mort
plutot que l'exclavage.

Voltaire.

51. *Brutus, c.* 1794. J. B. Vérité.

trate who could look down on current events from the Olympian heights of past time and moral rectitude. His only quality that could be construed in other times as a flaw was now a virtue: his nearly inhuman devotion to state law. When the Section de Brutus had to disband its executive committee, it told the Convention, 'Still worthy of the illustrious Roman whose name and whose feelings she had adopted, [the Section] will, as he did, sacrifice to the Fatherland everything she values the most.'[109] The chilling enthusiasm for such sacrifices is found in contemporary broadsides, one of which [50] adapts the famous line from Voltaire's play by changing Rome to France: 'Father, son, I will immolate everything I value the most to the well-being of my country, and like Brutus I will say after this sacrifice: *France is free, that suffices; let us give thanks to the gods.*'

It would be hard to exaggerate the prevalence of Brutus in 1793 and 1794. The central impulse had come from the Jacobins whose meeting places throughout France were guarded by his bust, and who had favored his presence before the speakers' rostrum in the Convention. The Convention encouraged the distribution of his image, and sponsored replicas in Sèvres porcelain,[110] plaster, and engravings. The Revolutionary tribunals had busts of Brutus, and he was regularly appealed to in judgments, both for and against the accused.[111] Many patriots changed their names to Brutus, and in the Paris region alone, some three hundred newborn children were registered with the first name Brutus.[112]

None of the plaster busts of Brutus seems to have survived, but there is no lack of prints from the period. Vérité's stipple engraving [51] is one of the more sophisticated. It is based on the Capitoline Brutus, and bears the popular cry from Voltaire's play, 'Gods! give us death rather than slavery'. Tiny engravings were made [52] to be pasted on buttons and on badges worn during the festivals. Even playing cards were redesigned. A conference of makers of popular broadsides agreed in February 1794[113] upon a common set of images to supplant the old 'monarchist' deck [53]. Kings became

52. *Brutus* and *Marat*, *c.* 1793–4. Anonymous.

the Sages, including Brutus, queens were now the Virtues, and knaves, the Warriors. Many printmakers announced suites of portrait-medallions whose pantheon usually consisted of Brutus, Voltaire, Rousseau, Franklin, Marat, Lepeletier and Chalier.

In the provinces, the extension of Jacobin power was accompanied by the same fervor for Brutus. Fréron, Barras and other emissaries of the Convention implanted the Brutus image as they travelled through the country. To rally the radical forces, they arranged festivals and ceremonies in which Brutus always had a prominent place, such as the inauguration of his bust in the secularized cathedral of Nevers on 21 September 1793, or the festival of 30 November at Marseilles, the climax of which was the presentation of Voltaire's *Brutus*. So important was the educational function of the play that Marseilles had the actors take the same oath of public duty required of teachers.[114] At Metz the next year, the guillotine was accompanied with a banner which substituted Metz for Rome in the lines from Voltaire, 'If in the streets of Metz there be a traitor . . .'[115]

Some of the regional clubs were led by reincarnations of the ancient Roman. The Revolutionary Military Commission at Rennes published a poster on 29 December 1793 signed by 'LP.B.BRUTUS MAGNIER, Président. SCEVOLA, Secrétaire-Greffier'. The extent of the cult of Brutus is indicated by the many villages and townships which changed their names. Ris-Orangis celebrated its new name 'Brutus' by holding a festival in November 1793, in which the bust of Brutus was carried on a Chariot of Liberty and then installed on a special village monument.[116]

The visual arts, the theatre and public formalities were consciously used for the purposes of public education by radical societies throughout France, partly at the behest of the two committees David served on, the Committee of Public Instruction and the Committee of Public Safety. For a population that was largely illiterate, these forms of communication were all the more urgently needed, and were susceptible of ready invention and quick produc-

53. Playing Cards of the Revolution, 1794. J. Minot.

108

tion. The Committee of Public Safety even brought and distributed popular broadsides – perhaps illustration 50 is one of them – and commissioned caricatures.

David himself proposed to the Committee two anti-British caricatures in May 1794 [54, 55] in response to its earlier invitation 'to multiply caricatures which can awaken the public spirit, and make it feel how atrocious and ridiculous are the enemies of Liberty and of the Republic'.[117] To give the impression that his cartoons were works emanating from the popular printmakers, they were not signed, and were carried out in the customary crude manner of the broadside artists.

The more permanent forms of visual art, painting and sculpture, tended to suffer in this volatile era, but we have some evidence of David's aspirations, at least. On 15 November 1793, the day after

54. *The Army of Jugs*, 1794. Broadside by David.

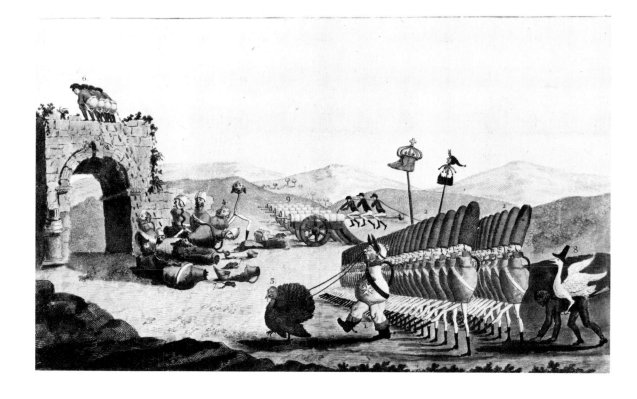

he had delivered his *Marat* and *Lepeletier* to the Convention, he offered his report on the *Jury des Arts*, whose task was to judge the new prize competition which replaced that of the defunct Academy.[118] (The subject, not surprisingly, was Brutus, and probably David's own choice.)

'It is not only in pleasing the eye that monuments of art attain their goal, it is in penetrating the soul, it is in making on the mind a profound impression, similar to reality. Then it is that marks of heroism, of civic virtues, offered to the people, will electrify their souls and implant in them all the passions of glory and devotion to the well-being of the Fatherland. It is therefore necessary that the artist study all the springs of the human heart. He must have a great knowledge of nature, in a word, he must be a philosopher. Socrates, skilful sculptor, Jean-Jacques, good musician, the immortal Poussin,

55. *The English Government*, 1794. Broadside by David.

tracing on his canvas the most sublime lessons of philosophy, are as so many witnesses who prove that the spirit of the arts should have as only guide the torch of reason.'

The 'torch of reason' is a phrase which includes the apparent opposites of passion and reason from which David had forged his style, and which he now held forth as the standard for a national art. It was not just an outburst of patriotic passion he favored, but passion annealed in the chamber of discipline. A practical demonstration was given that same month when he proposed a gigantic Statue of the People for the Île de la Cité. He had the Convention decree two competitions, one for the conception and another for the execution.[119] 'But the man who conceives the best is not always the one who executes the best. Genius conceives rapidly, the instant of creation is imperceptible, it is a streak of light, a sudden illumination. In execution, on the other hand, a continuous heat is needed, an impassioned slowness, an enthusiasm held by patience.'

This kind of taut passion is evident in a rare work by David that survives from the Terror [56], an unfinished project for an opera

56. *Triumph of the People*, *c.* 1793–4. David.

57 (*right*). Detail of 56.

curtain which must date from late 1793 or the first half of 1794. The chariot of the people rides over attributes of royalty, feudalism and theocracy, while Victory floats above the *sans-culottes* who are dispatching the league of monarchs. Accompanying the chariot are Cornelia and the two Gracchi, Brutus, Marat and Lepeletier, who show their wounds, William Tell, Chalier and others. Brutus [57] holds a sheet reading 'to death shall my sons be led', a direct citation from Voltaire's play (no other writer used those exact words). The whole is put together with 'impassioned slowness'. Borrowings from antiquity (the seated Hercules is a quotation from the famous Gemma Augustaea) and contemporary martyrs are amalgamated into a processional order recalling the festivals David designed.

The greatest of David's enterprises of 1794 is the Festival of the Supreme Being of 8 June, which he organized in conjunction with Robespierre, to celebrate the deistic religion calculated to weld together the disparate strands of the Revolution.[120] 'L'aurore annonce à peine le jour' begins in musical intonation this handsomest of David's programs.

'Dawn has barely announced the coming day when already the sounds of a warlike music reverberate from all sides, and to the calm of sleep bring an enchanting awakening.

At the sight of the beneficent star which vivifies and colors nature, friends, brothers, spouses, patriarchs and mothers embrace and eagerly hurry to decorate and celebrate the feast of the Divinity.'

The popular arts of the period do not reflect this festival very accurately, but some of them capture the mood. In one broadside [58] we find David's 'beneficent star' above an appeal to the Supreme Being. Rousseau is seated to the right, with children and a beehive to symbolize his position as man of nature. On the other side Voltaire stands near attributes of his writings, the most prominent of which is a bust of Brutus whose pedestal bears the now familiar 'Gods! give us death rather than slavery!'

58. *Voltaire and Rousseau Honoring the Supreme Being*, 1794. Anonymous.

At the height of the celebration of the Supreme Being, David had fathers and sons stand on one side of the artificial mountain constructed for the festival, and women and children on the other, separating the sexes as he had done in his paintings of *Brutus* and the Horaces. Daughters sing in honor of nature, and mothers of sons who conquer the tyrants leagued against the Republic. At the climactic moment, mothers raise their infants to the sky, girls throw their flowers toward the beneficent star, and 'simultaneously, the sons, burning with a warlike ardour, draw their swords from the hands of their venerable fathers; swearing to render them everywhere victorious, swearing to make equality and liberty triumph over oppression of tyrants.' We might almost think we were looking back upon the *Oath of the Horatii* [1] were it not for the 'formidable discharge of artillery, interpreter of national vengeance' which followed, and the reply of 'a virile and warlike song, prelude of victory'.

5. Brutus after Thermidor:
Napoleon and Exile

Robespierre had been able to congratulate himself in the late spring of 1794, and he could associate David with the good fortune of his policies. Revolutionary arms had held Europe at bay, internal enemies had been overcome, and the Revolution had proved that moral and political change could be enforced.

'Do not say, O Brutus, that virtue is a phantom! And you, founders of the French republic, beware of despairing of humanity, or of doubting for one moment the success of your great enterprise. The world has changed, it must change some more. What is there in common between what is, and what was? ... Compare the imperfect language of hieroglyphs with the miracles of printing ...; measure the distance between the astronomical observations of the magi from Asia and the discoveries of Newton, or further, between the rough sketch from the hand of Dibutade and the paintings by David.'[121]

But David, as well as Robespierre, fell from these heights in the debacle of 9th Thermidor, and although he kept his life, his art was no longer at the service of Revolution. While he languished in prison in the autumn of 1794, there were signs already of the recent past being overturned. An engraving was published [59] which showed sympathy for Louis XVI and his family, and which carica-tured the *sans-culotte* leading him to execution. What is more, the composition is a remaking of David's *Brutus*, a reversal of fortunes in which Brutus has become the king and Brutus's wife, children and servant have become the royal family.

59. *Louis XVI separated from his Family*, 1794. After P. Bouillon.

David was released from prison in 1795, but he lived a very private life, since the Directory could hardly be expected to honor the man who was Robespierre's favorite artist. A half-decade later David again found himself near the center of political power, but his admiration of Napoleon (never fully reciprocated, one feels) did not lead to the full engagement of his art and life which marks the Jacobin period.[122]

The Directory, however, although it eliminated Robespierre and pushed David into the shadows, was still a revolutionary coalition and passed on to the Consulate many of the characteristic features of the earlier period. Napoleon eventually transformed them, as we know, but not before some of them had their last, occasionally glorious celebrations. Among these is the cult of Brutus, which survived, even if with diminished vigor, until the Emperor exiled the Roman consul to the marmoreal silence of imperial halls and museums.

Voltaire's *Brutus* had suffered something of an eclipse in the last months of the Terror which foretold its eventual disappearance from the stage. Its last presentation in Paris was in 1799.[123] The demise of the play had several causes. Its strength had been the dialogue between tyranny and liberty, but a decade of public rhetoric had made that theme seem tiresome, and the play has insufficient dramatic value to sustain it on other grounds. The mood of Paris had altered, so that the starkness and frugality of the play, which so well suited the early Revolution, were no longer welcome, and the public executions which it had featured on stage were better forgotten, in light of those that had actually taken place. Besides, Napoleon might wish an identification with the founder of liberty, but he was not going to favor a play whose central attack was on the arbitrary exercise of power. An altogether more fitting classical symbol from the early Revolution were the white robes women wore, inspired by David's costumes and those of Talma's theatrical troupe. These robes were subsequently called 'Empire' style, one of the more harmless of Napoleon's usurpations.[124]

60. *Brutus*, 1794–5. After Molenchon.

The sculpted and painted image of Brutus was a bit more tenacious than the play, but essentially suffered the same fate. Under the last months of the Terror, Marat's bust had even displaced Brutus's in front of the speakers' rostrum in the Convention. Through 1795 and 1796, however, Brutus was still commonly found in painting, sculpture and the graphic arts. In April 1795 the Government paid for an order earlier given to the engraver Audouin for a thousand impressions of a drawing of Brutus by Molenchon [60]. It is a handsome print, one of the few that echo David's painting more than the Capitoline sculpture. Of about the same period is the medallion engraving by Louis Darcis after Lethière [61] which stresses the eagle-like aloofness of Brutus in its craggy outline. In

61. *Brutus, c.* 1795–6. After Lethière.

1796 the new National Institute of Sciences and Arts gave as prize a medal after the Capitoline head by Rambert Dumarest, and in the late 1790s, some military commanders and government functionaries included Brutus in their letterhead-vignettes.[125] The only major commission of the period in which Brutus figured was that for the Council of Five Hundred which was installed in the Palais Bourbon in January 1798. Six large plaster statues had been placed in niches: Brutus, Lycurgus, Cato, Cicero, Solon and Demosthenes. *Brutus* [62] was by Frédéric Lemot, and it was given the highest praise by the young Amaury-Duval,[126] although it was never rendered in stone, as intended. It was the last time a French government commissioned a public work devoted to Brutus.

The Capitoline bust of Brutus, meanwhile, continued to claim attention. When the Pope signed the armistice with the French in June 1796, he agreed to give a hundred works of art as reparations, and the first one named was the bust of Brutus from the Capitoline.[127] It was given very special care, and was separately noted in dispatches to Paris in 1797 when the art convoy left Rome. It took a central place in the last great festival of the Revolution, the 'Festival of Liberty and of the Triumphal Entry of Objects of the Arts and Sciences Gathered in Italy' held on 9th and 10th Thermidor l'an VI (27 and 28 July 1798), in commemoration of the defeat of Robespierre's tyranny.[128] The repeated refrain of the festival's music 'Rome is no longer in Rome, she belongs to Paris', was a triumphal fulfilment of the prediction of November 1790 when David had placed his copy of the Capitoline sculpture on the stage of Voltaire's play, and the actor playing Brutus had exclaimed

> *O honored bust of Brutus, of a great man,*
> *Brought to Paris, you have not left Rome.*

Brutus was carried on his own wagon of the fine arts section of the long parade. Preceded by a banner reading 'Artists hurry! Here are your masters!', the section included such memorable works as the *Capitoline Venus*, the *Apollo Belvedere*, the *Laocöon*, and Raphael's *Transfiguration*. On the pedestal bearing Brutus was inscribed from Tacitus: 'Rome was first governed by kings. Junius Brutus gave her liberty and the Republic', and on the wagon, the last line from Voltaire's play, 'Rome is free, that suffices, let us give thanks to the gods'. At the climax of the festival, the wagons with their works of art and their great books on science and philosophy were grouped on the Champ-de-Mars. Representatives of the nation gathered by a bust of Homer and a statue of Liberty, and a delegation solemnly placed the bust of Brutus on a special pedestal. On the second day of the festival, the members of the Directory descended the Altar of the Fatherland to pay homage to the bust of the first Roman consul by crowning it with laurel branches, sure in

62. *Brutus*, 1798. F. Lemot.

their conviction that France had seized not works of art, but the very spirit of the Roman republic.

The fate of Brutus's bust thereafter followed that of the republican spirit: both succumbed to Empire. In 1800 Bonaparte asked David to place the Capitoline head in the Tuileries, to join other great men there.[129] But Napoleon's identification with past heroes lay in other directions. He was Caesar, returning from Italy to govern Gaul; he was Augustus, leading expeditions to the Near East; he was Charlemagne, ruler of a new Holy Empire; he was Henry IV, in Voltaire's phrases 'pacifier of factions' and of his subjects both 'conqueror and father'.[130]

After Waterloo, when the Empire was dismantled, the monarchy restored, and the Capitoline bust returned to Rome, the remarkable second life of Brutus was at an end. In retrospect we can see why the first consul of Rome was such an enduring hero of the Revolution. He could survive the several changes of government because his legend lent itself to varied interpretations. By comparison, Caesar's Brutus was rather like Mucius Scaevola, associated with a single act and therefore lacking the many dimensions of the elder Brutus (besides, Marcus Brutus had not been *successful*). The first Brutus was in succession the defender of woman's virtue, the father who could sacrifice family to state honor, the opponent of royal tyranny and leader of rebellious forces, the upholder of new laws, and the unyielding judge of state enemies. No other antique hero could have rivalled him in responding to such complex and urgent needs, especially after Voltaire and David had provided him with such memorable images and words.[131]

Voltaire's play forgotten, and David himself in exile after Waterloo, what of the great painting of Brutus? Along with the *Horatii* it had been moved from David's studio to the new Senate Gallery in 1803, and ever since it has been in the national collections. Plekhanov could later recommend that young revolutionaries go to the Louvre to bow before the picture, but modern youth is no respecter of antiquity, and David's painting is admired by very few.

When the handsome new installations were underway in the Louvre in 1969, one could examine the back of the huge picture. In an over-size cursive hand, in dark ink, probably dating from 1820s or 1830s, was the inscription

ce tableau a été fait dans
le tems de la Révolution de
L'année 1789.

Appendix

[Note: For short titles, see Bibliography; translations are the author's; except for the Cuvillier letter, which is given in its entirety, all citations are excerpts from the originals, but only interior omissions are noted by ellipses.]

DAVID LETTER TO WICAR, 14 JUNE 1789. The original is in the École des Beaux-Arts, Paris, and given in facsimile in David Jules, foll. p. 622.

Finally there you are in Florence. Florence, think of it, the homeland of Michelangelo. Remember how little time he spent learning how to paint. Feeling and composition [*dessin*], there are the real masters for learning how to stir the brush. What does it matter if one makes strokes to the right, to the left, up and down or sideways; as long as the lights are in their places, one will always paint well. Misfortune to the one who says he does not know how to paint, meaning that he does not know how to blend [*fondre*]; that kind will never paint, even when he learns how to blend. He would not say that if he had what we mean by 'feeling'. For example, the great Guido [Reni], so highly esteemed by us in particular, I do not like him myself; I find him just a blender, and his heads do not at all have what I demand. I mean Guido generally speaking, for there are certain paintings of his that I admire.

And Fra Bartolommeo, speaking of this, what a man that one is! What heads of old men! Oh Florence! Florence! How far you are from Paris! Florence! Florence! You are there, so profit by it.

I am busy with a new painting, wretched as I feel. I am in this poor country like a dog thrown into the water against his will, and who has to reach the bank in order not to lose his life. And I, in order not to lose the little that I brought back from Italy, I try to keep myself up, and he who only sustains himself is close to dropping behind. But I also count on seeing soon again both Florence and Rome . . . When I have decided, I will inform you.

So I was about to say that I am doing a painting of my own invention. It is Brutus, man and father, who has deprived himself of his children and who has returned to his home, where are brought to him the bodies of his two sons for burial. He is interrupted in his distress, at the foot of the statue of Rome, by the cries of his wife, the fear and the fainting of his eldest daughter. The description is beautiful, but as for the painting, I do not dare say anything yet. It seems, not to lie to you, that they are content with the composition, but I, I do not dare say [illegible]. You would do me a favor to sketch on this [illegible] head a coiffure in the position that I indicate. It seems to me that you will find it among the Bacchanales. One often sees certain Bacchantes with such poses. But no matter, as long as you send me the dishevelled coiffure of a young girl, a coiffure in the style [i.e., of antiquity]. You do not have to make me a finished drawing, I will not take advantage of you like that. Besides, I only need the outline, in which one distinguishes well the masses of hair.

DAVID LETTER TO WICAR, 17 SEPTEMBER 1789. The original is in the Fondation Custodia, Paris.

I have just exhibited my *Brutus* in the Salon. It seems to me that of all my paintings it is the one which up to now has made the most fuss. I am covered in praises, but I am careful to take only what is proper. I do not often let myself be carried away by such language. It encourages me, that is all. They praise principally the conception [*la pensée*] and especially placing him in shadow. There is something Florentine in the rendering of my Brutus. You will see it one day, no need to say more. I did my best, that is all I can assure you of.

CUVILLIER LETTER TO VIEN, 10 AUGUST 1789. In Correspondance, no. 763, pp. 263-65.

Versailles, 10 August 1789

At our last meeting, Monsieur, about the coming opening of the Salon, the idea of which preoccupies Monsieur the General Director almost as much as making use of the waters, I expressed to you the justified and entire confidence he places in the prudence and caution of the Academy in organizing this Salon. I will not repeat here the reasons and the motives that unhesitatingly determine Monsieur the General Director to deprive neither the capital nor the artists of an event interesting for the pleasures of the former, valuable for the glory of the latter, and which, in the present moment, can serve morale as a useful diversion. None of that will have escaped your notice and will be equally understood by Messieurs of the Academy, hence it is only in a certain measure to complete the instructions prepared by Monsieur the General Director that I will offer a few observations here.

Monsieur the General Director thinks that one could not exercise too much caution in the choice of subjects which will be exhibited, relative to the interpretations which might escape from an observer and which could be awakened by others. The theatre provides us each day with the most unexpected examples. I only feel all the more how difficult it is to predict all that might be imagined, and my unique aim is to urge the committee to use all possible precaution.

The heading of portraits lets one more readily put oneself on guard, because in general the sitters being known, one is in the position of measuring public opinion and of not risking anything; I imagine that concerning this, M. Lavoisier will be the first to wish not to show his portrait. It is not that he could in any sense be ranked among those whom one could think badly of, but one can let him judge that. On the subject of portraits I am inclined to fear that Monsieur de Tollendal might renew the project of exhibiting this terrifying painting which it was so difficult to set aside in 1787; but, at the same time, I am reassured by the very virtue of Monsieur de Tollendal and by the loftiness of his views which will let him see at a glance the danger of furnishing more food to the fermentation. It is in this regard that I am comforted, as much as I could be, by learning that Monsieur David's painting is still far from finished; and, à propos this artist, I think as you, Monsieur, that his painting of *Paris and Helen* can be exhibited without remaining fears, by suppressing the owner's name. In this the only concern I see is the glory of the Academy and that of the artist.

I ought to express very particularly to you, Monsieur, the really deep distress which Monsieur the General Director would feel at the decision some of the artists might take not to contribute to the exhibition, and Monsieur the General Director urges you to press them on his behalf not to follow that course. In case there were too much empty space, the precise wish of Monsieur the General Director is that it be occupied by paintings sent to previous exhibitions that were not seen, or poorly seen. Messieurs *Roslin* and *Durameau* are in a position to respond to both cases, and I rely on them to be ready for the next committee meeting.

I have the honor, etc.

CUVILLIER

P.S. – Will you permit me to make the personal observation that it will perhaps be well to arrange the pictures so that the little ones will not be within reach of certain hands?

126

SALON 1789: *Mercure de France*, I, 24 October 1789.

We could have published earlier the review we are now going to give, but it would have been necessary to return to the lacunae in the exhibition, and the space that political subjects leave to literature and the arts is too shrunken to permit more than one article on a given theme. The one about to be read has little, very little criticism. It is not in the midst of troubles and uneasiness that artists can maintain that calm reflection which leads them to understand their imperfections or to recognize the soundness of the observations offered them. This article should therefore be considered only an homage to some talents . . .

[*Brutus:*] The style of this painting is male, severe, terrifying, and its oppositions are perfect . . . [Putting Brutus in shadow is an idea that is] new and grand, it adds to the character the painter has given Brutus, it completes the severity and the effect of the situation . . .

It is possible that we have passed over in silence some paintings hung towards the end of the exhibition, but at that time public troubles distracted everyone's mind from the concentration that the arts require of those who are encharged with the public recording of their opinions . . .

SALON 1789: *Affiches*, 260, 17 September 1789, p. 2657.

M. David, whose name suffices to attract the attention of connoisseurs, carries away all the honors again this year. His *Brutus* . . . is a composition of an absolutely new kind, one whose style is noble, severe, energetic, and one which retraces in the most suitable fashion a scene as touching as it is terrifying. The idea of placing Brutus absolutely in shadow is a stroke of genius, which helps render the figure sinister and sets off the interesting group formed by the mother and the sisters of the unfortunate victims of paternal severity.

SALON 1789: *Journal de Paris*, 312, 8 November 1789, p. 1450, in Deloynes, 16, no. 421.

The idea of this painting seems sublime to me, and also of the greatest interest. History belongs in the same manner to painter and to poet. Both have the right to create the circumstances which suit them. Monsieur David has created the action that he represents and, according to me, that is an additional merit.

SALON 1789: *Année littéraire*, 6, 1789, pp. 29f., in Deloynes, 16, no. 422.

The scene takes place in the interior of Brutus's home. His wife and his daughters give themselves up to despair when they see the bloody

bodies borne by the lictors, while Brutus tries to hide from the frightful
sight. One is familiar with the energetic expression, the pure and correct
drawing, and the enchanting and vigorous coloring of M. David, but it
is a pity that the beauties one finds in this subject – and there are very
great ones – should be obscured by faults which partly destroy them.
More than half the painting, where Brutus is found, is so dark that one
barely makes out the consul's pose. Would M. David have feared his
inability to express Brutus's suffering, and would he have thought of
using the known strategy of a painter of antiquity who, despairing of
expressing Agamemnon's grief, hid his face with his cloak? The group
of women is well chosen, in the antique style. It is perfectly correct, but
the contours are cold.

SALON 1789: *Supplément aux Remarques sur les ouvrages exposés au
Salon par le C. de MM.* [i.e., Comte de Mende Maupas], in Deloynes,
16, no. 414.

To appreciate the sublime beauties of this composition, one must go
back to the time when Rome built its liberty on the coarseness of its
customs, when would-be citizens only dethroned kings in order to reign
themselves, when natural feelings gave way to ardent ambition, when a
republican phantom consoled the people for the tyranny of its consuls.
Then one will understand the merits of M. David's painting: strength of
composition, nobility of expression, decisiveness of movement, agony of
pose and, more than all that, originality of conception, because the principal subject is found in the dark portion of the picture, as though to mark
the suffering of a being whom the republican morgue cannot prevent from
being a father. In effect this production is more that of a great poet than
of a painter, and the reproach that I heard *of seeing two paintings in the
subject* is the very cause of my admiration. I think I see J. Brutus,
removing himself from this family, but not yet reproaching himself for
his severity; I think I see him wavering between nature and ambition,
hence I admire this painting. But, since my enthusiasm never blinds me,
I think I should remark to the celebrated M. David that the uncertainty
of the light in this painting could serve as pretext for the criticism of
envious and malicious mediocrity.

SALON 1789: *Lettre des graveurs de Paris . . .* , in Deloynes, 16, no. 426.

It seems that with the cries of his wife Brutus feels all the loss he has
caused in sacrificing his two sons, and one imagines him listening to
these two beautiful verses that Racine put in the mouth of Agamemnon,

Voilà, voilà les cris que je craignais d'entendre . . . hélas!
en m'imposant une loi si sévère,
Grands Dieux! me devicé-vous: laisser un coeur de père.

However the positions of these two fathers were so different! The tender Iphigenia died innocent, but the sons of Brutus had conspired against the liberty their father had just given his fatherland by expelling the Tarquins. Also, when one tells Junius Brutus that his sons have died by his order, Voltaire has him say proudly,

Rome est libre, il suffit; rendons grâces aux Dieux!

Amateurs of picturesque liaison have found that the three groups which formed M. David's composition were too separated, and produced three pictures, but the young sister who faints on her mother's bosom is a sublime figure who compensates for such faults or even worse ones, if such there be in the work of this talented artist . . .

SALON 1789: Grimm, 'Suite du Salon de 1789', in Grimm, 15, pp. 535ff.

Brutus is seated in shadow at the foot of a statue in Etruscan style repre-senting Roma; he still holds in his hand the decree of the Senate granting him the right to judge his two sons [error: Brutus holds the traitors' letter to Tarquin]. His whole attitude and expression bear at the same time marks of a profound affliction and of an inflexible severity. 'I have had to accomplish it, this cruel sacrifice': that is the feeling which seems to be impressed on his lips, but with a sombre and withdrawn grief which is sufficient evidence of all the force and constancy he had to muster in order to win so painful a victory, in order to sustain so heroic a devotion, *eminente animo patrio inter publicae poenae ministerium.* [Livy, II, v]. This austere figure, isolated and as it were enshrouded in shadows, forms an admirable contrast with this group of women, illuminated by a light that is rather bright, but gentle and tranquil. It is Brutus's wife with her two daughters, her arms stretched sorrowfully towards the bodies of her two sons which the lictors return to the place destined for their burial. One of the daughters falls in a faint on her mother's breast, the other seems to have wished to follow longer with her eyes these cherished remains, but she does not have the energy; her hands, placed in front of her face, push away the frightful sight. . . Several have observed that in this painting there are two separate scenes, the worst fault one could reproach a work of this sort with, and we agree that before having been able to grasp the whole conception of the artist, the eye is in some fashion offended by this singular separation of light and dark which, one might say, divides the canvas in two entirely different parts. However, with steady attention one soon sees the intimate connection of the two scenes, and one can no longer doubt that the action is unequivocally unified, and thanks to the double scene our interest, without ceasing to be concentrated, is only the more lively and moving.

VON HALEM IN 1790: Von Halem, after visiting David's studio in 1790, in Von Halem, pp. 237f.

Several painters have already treated this subject, but each differed by the choice of the moment. [F. H.] Füger represented the instant between the sentence and the execution: the sons are taken to the block, but the supplicating stares of the onlookers, fixed on the father, let one hope still for a reprieve. The second painter who dared broach the subject, [G. G.] Lethière, tried to remove this hope and already showed the bloody head of one son. But one flees before blood and one suffers the double fear that the blood of the second son will be shed or that it will not be . . . David has made the best choice. He has opted for the moment which follows the execution, and yet he has spared us the horrible sight of the place of execution. Brutus, who suffers internally . . . understands everything, and keeps quiet. A thought furrows his brow. Ah! if the twilight which envelops me would change to darkness! He swallows his suffering, convulsive movements shake him even to his extremities, and his feet are twisting . . . And moreover, the spectator ought not to doubt for a moment that the wretched one suffers because he is aware of a bad action.

SALON 1791: Anonymous, *Explication et critique impartiale de toutes les peintures, sculptures . . . exposés au Louvre . . . au mois de Septembre 1791, l'an IIIe de la Liberté*, in Deloynes, 17, no. 436.

Everyone knows this painting. The composition is imposing, a sad and lugubrious silence reigns there. It casts blackness [*Il jette du noir*] into the soul of him who contemplates it. The drawing is pure and correct; it is well painted and makes an impression, but the figures seem a bit too much cut out against the background, which is too dark.

SALON 1791: Pithou, *Le Plaisir prolongé, le retour du Salon*, Paris, 1791, in Deloynes, 17, no. 437.

Brutus, your virtue has cost you dearly, but you owe this terrifying example to your fellow citizens.

How sombre he is! How he is crushed with pain! Ah! here is the funeral: desolate family, impressionable sisters, shed, shed your torrents of tears. Rome pities you, but Rome will inscribe these words in marble: *To Brutus, who sacrificed his children to his grateful Fatherland.*

SALON 1791: Anonymous, *La Béquille de Voltaire au Salon, Seconde et dernière promenade* . . . , Paris, 1791, in Deloynes, 17, no. 439.

This sublime composition seizes the soul at the first approach: one despairs with the mother, one is moved to pity with the daughters, one groans over the sons' fate, one shudders with the father. But, returning to one's senses, one finds that the painting, which seems cut in two parts, seems to form two subjects. One might also wish that the young girl who, *aided by her spread hands* wishes to hide from the sight *which she looks at,* might instead turn her head to the other side.

SALON 1791: Anonymous, *Lettres critiques sur les tableaux du Salon de 1791*, Paris, 1791, in Deloynes, 17, no. 441. The author is so biased against David that his words must be read with caution.

[*Brutus:*] Another painting by Monsieur David, much more improbable than the *Oath of the Horatii* because, without doing violence to all natural proprieties, one cannot imagine that Brutus, after having his sons butchered, would have withdrawn immediately to the room where his mother, wife and two daughters were working, nor that then the bodies of the two sons would have been brought through this same room in order to give them burial. One readily sees in this last circumstance that this subject is a pure invention and that the artist was not instructed in antique customs, because all the historians back to the poets say expressly that burials did not take place in cities. . . Thus it was unlikely that the sons of Brutus would have been brought into the house and through the room only later to have them borne out of the city. If a play were filled with so much disjointedness it would not be bearable, but anything goes in painting because one does not have the habit of searching beyond the picture.

Let us consider each figure one at a time, and let us begin with Brutus. The conception is beautiful, but is it M. David's? That is what we shall learn. *Lucius Junius Brutus*, to avoid the sentence Tarquin had pronounced against his family, withdrew into himself and only showed a rough exterior, like the stick he put in the Delphic temple in which he had hidden a golden rod. Such a man stands too far apart from other men to be confused with them. If M. David thought thus, he thought correctly, and he will therefore have said: I have no choice but to have recourse to Raphael, and I will appropriate his idea by applying it to Brutus.

Raphael, he would have said, wishing to express that the character of Diogenes, who had pushed from his presence a vile brigand soiled in crime, differed from that of the other philosophers, flung him down alone in the middle of the School of Athens, and by this ingenious idea gave a physical rendering to his moral nature. Very well! I will paint Brutus alone. He was of sombre character, very well! let us place him in the shadows, and there is moral Brutus by way of physical Brutus. And now where does the pose come from? Oh, you are going to recognize it, my good friend. Open the volume containing the antique statues of the Villa Négroni, and to the figure called Sulla, and you will have Brutus with few differences. Is this figure of Brutus beautiful? The head has some expression, the feet are twisted and the left hand responds but the right ought to share in this crisis. Brutus leans on the statue of Rome, which for reasons I do not know is made to face the viewer and not the room, to which it turns its side.

The group of the mother and the two children is another theft from antique figures, except that here it is a mother who supports her daughter while stretching out her arm towards her son, while in the original it is an old man who catches in a vase, held in the same extended arm, some water coming out of a rock, in order to succour a young girl who falls exactly and fold by fold like M. David's.

I will not further extend my analysis of this picture, very inferior to the Horaces.

Notes

1. *Mercure de France*, 12, 4 December 1790, pp. 40 ff.
2. *Chronique de Paris*, 322, 18 November 1790, pp. 1286 ff.
3. Grimm, p. 117. For short titles, see Bibliography.
4. For the elder Brutus the chief antique sources are Livy and Plutarch. In the eighteenth century, Rollin's *Histoire Romaine* (1738) was the most popular account. Marcus Brutus is better remembered today, but this was not so in the later eighteenth century, when Lucius Junius was associated with the successful overthrow of monarchy and the establishment of rule by *law*. Law and *sentiment*, those two leading characteristics of eighteenth-century France, were more perfectly embodied in the elder Brutus
5. Engerand, p. 138.
6. David Jules, p. 655.
7. Locquin and Rosenblum Transformations.
8. Louvre, Cabinet des dessins, R.F. 26092.
9. Such linking and flattening movements are carried out in small details. One is the continuation of the lines of the garment over the servant's knee with those of the wife's robe, the portion retained on the seat of the chair. Another is the addition of the sewing basket to the table, which keeps our eye from sinking back into space at that point, while also linking the chair and the women.
10. Adhémar Calques, pl. 109, n. 166, from the Capitoline.
11. Full text in Appendix (p. 123-4).
12. See, for example, the figure from the famous Medea sarcophagus in Mantua, of which David had made a copy: Adhémar Calques, pl. 201, no. 196. The perspicacious Robert Rosenblum (Transformations, p. 77) calls David's whole group 'hysterical bacchantes'.
13. *Discourses*, xii, cited appropriately enough by Darwin, Charles, *Expression of the Emotions in Man and Animals*, 1872, p. 208.
14. Hautecoeur, p. 100.
15. *L'Antiquité expliquée*, Paris, 1721, 1, pl. 87, 'an old picture in the Barberini palace'. The tracing after Brutus [16] has not before been correctly identified.
16. Louvre, Cabinet des dessins, R.F. 4506, p. 54 recto.

17. Louvre, Cabinet des dessins, R.F. 26109 quater. Hautecoeur confuses the two coiffures and thinks this the one David asked Wicar to sketch.

18. In Robert, Carl, *Die Antichen Sarkophag-Reliefs*, Berlin, 1919, 3, the Lateran example is no. 315 and the Vatican, no. 313 (uncovered in Rome in 1775, the year David arrived there). See also 316 and 317. Hautecoeur, p. 100, and others refer to the Uffizi's sculpture in the round of the Niobe group, but it seems less close to David.

19. Groups of grief-stricken women appear in a number of Roman reliefs of tragic theme, including the Rape of Proserpine and the Transportation of the Body of Hector. One of the best-known instances of the latter is the relief in the Villa Borghese in which the outstretched arms are the general prototype for the early version of Brutus's wife in David's drawings [4, 5, 7]. A tantalizing comparison of another kind was made by the anonymous author of *Lettres critiques* of 1791: see Appendix (p. 131).

20. Both cited by Hautecoeur, p. 100. The drawing for the first is in the Louvre, and there are tracings of both in Adhémar Calques, pls. 32 and 41.

21. Tikkanen, J. J., *Die Beinstellungen in der Kunstgeschichte*, Helsinki, 1912, p. 185 and *passim*, puts David's figure in this tradition. He introduces *Penelope* without making reference to *Brutus*.

22. Adhémar Calques, pl. 203, no. 194, not there identified; it is from the 'frieze of the Temple of Pallas' and reproduced in Montfaucon, op. cit., 1, pl. 15, and other repertoria of the eighteenth century.

23. Delécluze, p. 219 and *passim*, reports David's interest in early Renaissance art, and Honour pp. 36 ff., properly introduced Giotto, offering a marvelous discussion of the vital current of interest in early 'primitive' classicism. The comparison with Poussin has always been made, and has been summarized recently by Hazlehurst, F. H., 'The Artistic Evolution of David's *Oath*', *Art Bulletin*, 42, March 1960, pp. 59–63. Holma makes out a case for Raphael and has an ingenious, if finally unconvincing comparison of the *Fire in the Borgo* with *Brutus*. Raphael's importance for David seems most evident in the 1770s and early 1780s.

24. See the anthology of criticism in the Appendix. The citations which follow can readily be found there.

25. David Jules, p. 54.

26. The mathematical structure of *Brutus* is based on the Golden Section, or mean and extreme ratio, that is, the proportion admired from ancient times because of its elegant simplicity: the smaller of two parts is to the larger as the larger is to the sum of both ($A/B = B/A + B$). In *Brutus* the prominent left edge of the main column, half way up the picture, is precisely on the Golden Section. To its left, the resultant space is

exactly two squares high in proportion. To its right, a rectangle is formed such that its diagonals, swung from either corner on the right, would exactly determine the width (therefore the other corners) of the whole. The Golden Section division on the vertical is equally vital. The upper Golden horizontal (there are always two, since one can reverse the order of larger and smaller segments) crosses along the kneecap and toes of the body on the bier, through the eyes of the bearer, and touches the upper edge of the mother's outstretched thumb and the top of her head. The lower Golden horizontal follows the horizontal on which Brutus's elbow leans, the near edge of the central table, and the upper edge of the right-hand chair.

27. The comparison with Vignola was stated by Rosenthal, p. 37, and parallels with contemporary architecture by Crozet and Honour.

28. Delécluze, p. 114, notes David's preference in that regard when he first went to Rome. The *Saint-Roch* in Marseilles is a pastiche of sixteenth- and seventeenth-century work, including a direct borrowing from Caravaggio's *Boy Bitten by a Lizard* (Rome).

29. Lefebvre is still the best study of the period 1788-9.

30. In Brissot's *Le Patriote Français*, 1, 24 August 1789, p. 6, a contributor offered as object lesson the story of the anti-aristocrat, Caïus Gracchus, and in the *Révolutions de Paris* 10, 12-19 September 1789, p. 6, another citizen, writing of the plots of the émigrés, recalled the story of Mucius Scaevola (who had tried to kill Tarquin's ally Porsenna) and cried 'Frenchmen, cast your eyes on the great examples the Romans have given you!' There would have been no association of Tarquin, a particularly vicious murderer, with Louis XVI (that came three years later). The king was considered an ally of the reformers against unreconciled aristocrats. Desmoulins, in his pamphlet *La France Libre* of the summer of 1789 was virtually alone in attacking the principle of monarchy. 'Tarquin, cried Cicero, was not bad either. He was not cruel, he was only proud, and our ancestors expelled him. But they were Romans, and we . . . are worth more than the Romans.' (pp. 50 f.) In view of David's neoclassical style, it is instructive that Desmoulins used the pejorative 'Gothic' when writing of royalty, and evoked antiquity when writing of democracy.

31. *Histoire de la Société française pendant la Révolution*, pp. 43ff. This seems to be the origin of the misinterpretation, which is repeated by David Jules and by subsequent biographers, including Dowd 1948. My own skepticism came in a seminar in 1955, under John McCoubrey's guidance, when I failed to find any political interpretation of David's painting in the available Salon reviews. Robert Rosenblum came to the same view independently and discarded the old tradition in his several

publications concerning *Brutus*. Ettlinger debunked the political interpretation but went too far, perhaps as a result of our conversations together in the wake of seminars I had conducted at Yale. The revisionist thesis of Ettlinger and Honour will be discussed in due course.

32. The anonymous author of the Notice, p. 35, published while David was still alive.

33. Montaiglon, A. de, *Procès-verbaux de l'Académie Royale de Peinture et de Sculpture, 1648-1793*, Paris, 1892, 10, pp. 25-45, and discussed carefully in Dowd 1948, chapter II. Although he followed the Goncourts' error about the political reception of *Brutus*, Dowd offered by far the best interpretation of the way David's temperament and career before 1789 made logical his espousal of the Revolution.

34. *Journal de Paris*, 252, 9 September 1789, p. 1144. Mme Moitte, the organizer, published a pamphlet on the occasion called 'The Soul of Roman matrons in French Women'. Her collaborators, besides Mme David, included the wives of Vien, Suvée, Fragonard and LaGrenée the Younger. See Rosenblum Transformations, pp. 86f.

35. Locquin and Rosenblum Transformations.

36. Baron, Hans, *The Crisis of the Early Italian Renaissance*, Princeton, 1955.

37. Alfieri almost certainly knew David. See Boyer, Ferdinand, 'Vittorio Alfieri et les Beaux-Arts', *Atti del Quinto Congresso Internazionale di Lingue et Litterature Moderne*, 1955, pp. 279-84.

38. As is done by Ettlinger and by Sloane, Joseph, 'David, Robespierre and "The Death of Bara"', *Gazette des Beaux-Arts*, 6, 74, September 1969, pp. 143-57.

39. Rosenblum Transformations.

40. Sacy, Jacques Silvestre de, *Le Comte d'Angiviller*, Paris, 1953. In a revolution almost all gestures are political, and therefore the dedication to Angiviller which Peyron put on his engraving of 1790 [24] must have been a conscious royalist act.

41. Some lines seem to have been altered by Chénier after July 1789. Coligny is made to evoke the future destruction of the Bastille and the establishment of a liberal monarchy whose king will be the 'Restorer of law and of liberty'. The best general account of Chénier's play in the context of 1789 is in Dreyfous, and a more detailed one in Carlson. Neither exploits the rich documentation in the radical press of 1789 and 1790.

42. 1, 19 August 1789, p. 4.

43. Mention should also be made of the presentation on 22 September 1789 of the play *Raymonde V, Comte de Toulouse* by David's mentor and intimate family friend, Michel Sedaine. According to Sedaine himself, in a letter to the *Journal de Paris*, 267, 24 September 1789, p. 1217, the

play was refused in 1777 and had to await the new era to be shown. It is a comedy of manners whose 'political' side is simply the opposition of court intriguers to Raymonde's attempts to put on an amateur play. 'On a applaudi', wrote the reviewer for the *Mercure de France*, 3 October 1789, pp. 20 ff., 'quelques traits susceptibles d'applications, on en a reprouvé bien davantage.'

44. David's receipt is dated 16 December 1788: Fric, René, *Catalogue préliminaire de la correspondance de Lavoisier*, Paris, 1949, p. 53. For Lavoisier's life see the still basic Grimaux, Édouard, *Lavoisier 1743-1794*, Paris, 1896.

45. The de Wailly drawing is discussed, and many of the pictures identified, in Wilhelm, J., 'Un projet de Charles de Wailly pour l'aménagement du Salon du Louvre', *Bulletin du Musée Carnavalet*, 16 June 1963, pp. 5-10. The Lally-Tollendal portrait is just to the right of the archway, with *Paris and Helen* to its right. *Brutus* is above to the right, matched on the other side by Peyron's *Death of Socrates* [24]. In the extreme lower left is Vestier's portrait of Latude [32]. In addition to identifying the present location of the Robin portrait, one can add to Wilhelm's account that the de Wailly drawing was actually exhibited during the Salon and was favorably reviewed by *Le Spectateur français au Salon de 1789*, in Deloynes, 16, no. 424.

46. Popular fears of intrigue against the Assembly and the people pointed to intimates of the court, although the king himself was spared direct accusation, and the fears were fueled by the mounting wave of emigration of the aristocrats, who were believed to be seeking aid from neighbouring countries, as Tarquin had among Rome's enemies. On the very day of Cuvillier's letter, the press reported (*Révolutions de Paris*, 5, 9-16 August 1789, report dated 10 August) that the Comte d'Artois was selling his horses for cash and was about to leave for Italy. When the Salon opened on 25 August, there were widespread accounts of Artois seeking refuge in Switzerland.

47. Honour thought the unfinished painting was the Lavoisier portrait, but this had been completed the previous December.

48. Ettlinger argues that official opposition to *Brutus* was not on political grounds, but because the subject lacked prior approval (Coriolanus having been agreed upon), that this opposition was the reason for the picture's not being on exhibit when the Salon opened, and that David's fame forced its eventual acceptance. Perhaps this interpretation was inspired by Engerand who states wrongly that the *Brutus* was not considered a royal commission.

49. 'Brutus is not in the Salon,/And we know the reason./He wants us to be blasés/About the works on display/Before offering his work./ . . .

By this detour, adroitly, / This artist eludes the tooth / And the eye of the critic.': Anonymous, *Pensées d'un prisonnier de la Bastille sur les tableaux exposés au Salon du Louvre en 1789*, in Deloynes, 16, no. 411.

50. Ettlinger correctly discounts the views of Dowd 1948 and others that outraged public opinion forced the government to accept David's picture, and that his art students 'protected' the picture. As residents of the Louvre district, the art students had enrolled in Lafayette's popular militia and had asked to replace the customary Royal Swiss guard in the Salon: see the Cuvillier-Vien letters in Correspondance. They took over by 12 August, during the judging (Wille, p. 214) and might possibly have intimidated the jury. In September there had been open opposition from the Swiss guards, and there is no doubt that their presence was a political one – but *Brutus* had prior acceptance and their role was simply to maintain order in a time of near anarchy.

51. Would he have thought of the fact that Louis XVI was still mourning his son, who had died in June?

52. 3, undated, p. 10. The exact date becomes clear in the context.

53. *Éclaircissements adressés à l'auteur de la feuille intitulé 'L'Observateur No. 3'*, 'Versailles le 13 Août 1789, sept heures du soir', 'chez Baudouin. Imprimeur de l'Assemblée Nationale', signed simply 'Cuvillier'.

54. 4, undated, p. 22.

55. *L'Observateur* had also published in the rebuttal an account of the censorship of the Lally-Tollendal portrait in 1787. On 25 August when the Salon had finally opened, *l'Observateur* threw the same dart again. 'The public has seen again this year with satisfaction a portrait of M. le Comte de Lally-Tollendal, which two years ago had hardly appeared when it was removed by what one then called *higher orders*'. The *Chronique de Paris* (1, 24 August, p. 2), another radical journal, republished *l'Observateur*'s first exposé of attempted censorship and mentioned both David's *Brutus* and Barbier's portrait of the grenadier which had figured in the exchange between Cuvillier and the journal.

56. *Mémoires de Henri Masers de Latude* (ed. by Thiery), originally 1792, in *Bibliothèque des Mémoires* (ed. by F. Barrière), 28, Paris, 1866, p. 255.

57. 2, 25 August 1789, p. 18.

58. Recounted by the host's heir, C. Mellinet, in an essay several times reproduced in the 1830s, cited by Saunier, pp. 39f.

59. *Le Patriote Français*, 451, 2 November 1790, p. 2. David Jules, p. 90, and Dowd 1948, pp. 36ff., both refer to this incident but make no mention of Mirabeau and wrongly state that references were made to David's earlier pictures having foretold the Revolution. Von Halem

recounts a visit to David's studio in late October that seems to prove that David had already begun the picture before the public proposal was made (he might have inspired it, in fact). The gigantic picture was never completed.

60. 'Salon de 1791', in *Lettres choisies de Charles Villette*, Paris, 1792, p. 238. David was a member of the special commission which eliminated the restrictive rules governing the Salon. 'Patriotic' subjects such as allegories of liberty and of the Bastille were common, and still more numerous were works honoring Mirabeau, Voltaire and Rousseau. 'Francklin' was the subject of two sculptures, and another was listed as 'Allégories de Wasingthon [sic] et de la Liberté', that troublesome 'h' migrating even further than usual from its native syllable. Classical subjects were as common as before, but now no one was shy at calling attention to current interpretations. Berthélemy's *Manlius Torquatus Condemning his Son*, originally exhibited in 1785, was called 'a lesson to be reproduced today, because it is given by a free people' (*Chronique de Paris*, in Deloynes, 17, no. 452). Among other works were Peyron's engraving [24] after his earlier *Death of Socrates*, an engraving of an *Oath of the Horatii* by Carat, Lefebvre's *Death of Socrates*, and Vigniallis's *Brutus Condemning his Sons*.

61. Rockwood is the essential study of Voltaire in the period to 1791, although he does not include all of the testimony that I introduce.

62. Ar. Parl., 9, p. 182, for 25 September 1789.

63. *Chronique de Paris*, 46, 3 October 1789, p. 163. The *Mercure de France*, 17 October 1789, pp. 61-3, reviewed *Voltaire aux français sur leur constitution* (anonymous, but given to J. L. Laya), devoted to the relevance of Voltaire to the new liberty.

64. *Lettres des graveurs*, 1789, Appendix.

65. Mathiez, pp. 31f.

66. One of the best descriptions of the Confédération Nationale of 14 July 1790 is in *L'Ami du Roi*, 1, 19 July 1790, pp. 201f. The engraving of the altar [35] shows it with the addition in September 1790 of the monument to the soldiers killed at Nancy the previous month.

67. Rockwood, pp. 105f. Rockwood errs, however, as do Dowd 1948 and most others, in stating that there were only sixteen presentations of *Brutus* before the 'revival' of 1790. There were about ninety from 1730-86: Joannidès, A., *La Comédie française de 1680 à 1920*, Paris, 1921, p. 102. The error stems from the Revolutionary period which wanted to believe that *Brutus* had been suppressed under the monarchy. The edition of 1790 notes, 'This tragedy . . . was only played sixteen times . . . Its reprise in 1790 has made its beauty better felt. It proves that the collaboration of circumstances is needed in order to develop all the merits of certain works

that one is subsequently surprised at having neglected.' Initially guided by Rockwood and Dowd 1948, the account I give of the play is based principally upon these periodicals of November and December 1790: *Chronique de Paris*, *Journal Universel*, *Affiches*, *Mercure de France* and *Revolutions de Paris*, and by these witness accounts: Grimm and Von Halem. I include only those anecdotes reliably verified by more than one source.

68. To the extent that Voltaire's *Brutus* can be given a political reading, Ridgway offers the best interpretation.

69. A later engraving of the upper portion of the figure by H. B. Hall suggests that the picture was in Great Britain by the 1840s, but the artist remains unknown. It is also unclear whether the grisaille on the wall behind reproduces a real study by David (in this case, there is no other record), or whether it is an invention of the portraitist. The absence of the empty chair in the Brutus composition is hard to explain in either case.

70. Identification with Rome was felt particularly in the oath on the altar of Mars and its subsequent evocations in the play. In July 1790 there had been the oath on the Altar of the Fatherland, with its citations from Voltaire and its sculptures inspired by David's *Oath of the Horatii* [1]; in late October there came the proposal that David paint the oath in the Tennis Court; in early November Mirabeau and Brissot noted that David's *Horatii* had foretold the Tennis Court oath; on 1 December *Affiches* (335, pp. 3789 f.) wrote that '*The Oath of the Horatii* has such distinctive character that one cannot paint patriotic zeal and the civic oath without using the poses David gave them. His figures were copied and placed on the Altar of the Fatherland [35], raised on the Champ-de-Mars for the ceremony of the Pact of Unity . . .'

71. In Madeleine Scudéry's *Clélie* of 1661, Brutus tries to save his sons and only agrees to their execution when the populace forces the issue. In Nathaniel Lee's *Brutus* of 1680, Valerius stabs Titus at the end to spare him the ignominy of the axe! Lee invents the Romeo-Juliet plot in which Titus loves Tarquin's daughter, and he has a number of scenes in which Brutus's wife and Tarquin's daughter plead with the consul. The play was banned after six performances for its anti-monarchial sentiment. Catherine Bernard's *Brutus* of 1691 has the execution take place offstage in a play more devoted to love than to liberty. Voltaire borrowed extensively from Bernard (and some from Lee), but important as love is, it is part of the dialectic of love versus honor which marks the French tradition. Love is subordinated to the virtue of state-centered patriotism and to the lessons of humbled pride. Antonio Conti's *Bruto* of 1743 gives prominence to women pleading with Brutus, as Lee had done, and in this they both look forward to David's picture. When Conti's

Brutus gives his sons over to the lictors, his wife cries out 'Bruto, Bruto, / Figli, Littori, v' arrestate, oh Dio!'. and in other scenes of pleading she is accompanied by a veritable chorus of matrons. Alfieri's *Bruto Primo* of 1788 largely eliminates the women and attempts a stern interpretation, but his Brutus is rather teary, more pathetic than tragic. The erect head of David's figure credits him with an authority and an ability to suppress emotion which likens him more to Voltaire than to Alfieri. On David and contemporary theatre, see Dowd 1960.

72. *Brutus* has been presented two years out of every three since David's birth. The archives of the Comédie française show that the artist Brunetti had painted the décor for *Brutus* in 1769 to 1771, including 'a gilded altar very richly adorned with a statue of Mars', and that for the play there were 'two armchairs, two benches, a stool, on the royal side; an altar with a vessel of burning spirits in the middle of the theatre before the curtain rises. The statue of Mars and the Champ-de-Mars for the first act.'

73. The illustrations to Voltaire by Moreau-le-Jeune and Gravelot are a major source for David and later for Gros. David's *Socrates* might owe something to Moreau-le-Jeune's *Socrate* of 1785, and his *Sabines*, to the same artist's *Adelaide* of 1783. Gros's *Napoleon at Eylau* has major borrowings directly from Gravelot's *Henriade*.

74. Duval, Émile, *Talma, précis historique*, Paris (third edn.), 1826, p. 11. The best modern histories, Carlson and Collins, H. F., *Talma*, 1964, wrongly place the revival of *Brutus* in 1789. Talma, David's junior by eighteen years, had much of his temperament, and their careers offer striking analogies. He was a rebel against authority at an early age, complained of persecution, and led a dissident faction in the national theatre as David had in the Academy. He was among those (Talma, *Correspondance avec Madame de Staël*, Paris, 1928, letter of 25 December 1790) who demanded that *Brutus*, *Charles IX* and other 'democratic plays' be produced for the unity celebrations of 14 July 1790, and when he founded his schismatic Théâtre de la Rue de Richelieu in the spring of 1791, *Brutus* was among the first plays put on. It was produced with new settings and costumes, notable for their severe 'archeological' simplicity à la David. The archives of the Comédie française offer no details of the costumes for Talma's troupe, but include a lengthy set of extracts from books on Greek and Roman costume. The archives also show that from 1791 to 1799, Talma's sole role in the play was Titus. A later engraving for *Brutus* [38], apparently shows the costumes and the setting of the Revolutionary productions of the play, and incorporates a homage to David's painting. The Rondel collection (Bibliothèque de l'Arsenal) has a colored drawing of Talma in the role of Titus, and Moreau-le-Jeune's

illustration for Voltaire's play, engraved by Delvaux in the late 1790s, shows Brutus seated next to a statue of Rome, recalling David's picture.

75. Gravelle, E. des, *Lettre aux sections de Paris*, Paris, 1790, brochure of three pages.

76. Rockwood and McKee claim that the play's popularity has been exaggerated, but they do not take into account the large number of popular presentations outside the legitimate theatre nor even all the latter's, such as the Gaieté's performances of 1794. Their emphasis is sound, however, and *Brutus* appeared not much above two dozen times a year from 1791 to 1794, after which it dropped off sharply.

77. *Révolutions de Paris*, 2, 4–11 December 1790, pp. 445–55.

78. On 22 November 1790, at the third performance of *Brutus*, Charles Villette had renewed the proposal for a national homage to Voltaire. 'It is up to the Romans, to the Frenchmen such as you', he cried to the audience, to expiate the opposition to Voltaire by church and state by placing his remains in the new basilica dominating the Left Bank. He had already proposed that 'to bring us closer to the Greeks and Romans, from whom we hold so many maxims of liberty, to give an example to Europe, let us have the courage not to put this temple under the invocation of a saint. Let it be the *French Pantheon*.' The new building by Soufflot, largely finished but not yet consecrated to Ste Geneviève, was based on the classical tradition which Villette found appropriate to Voltaire, as distinct from 'Gothick' architecture which he associated with religion and royalty. Its Corinthian columns were a fitting 'image of his immortality' (*Chronique de Paris*, 329, 25 November 1790, p. 1314; 327, 23 November 1790, p. 1305, and 109, 21 December 1789, p. 478).

79. Aulard Histoire, p. 125. The poster declared that the Cordeliers were now tyrannicides who vowed to assassinate all tyrants who attack France or her new liberty, and in the Assembly there was announced simultaneously a similar group called 'Mucius Scaevola' (Buchez Roux, 10, p. 418). A number of theatres (including Talma's) had been playing *Brutus* since late May, but after the flight to Varennes, the presentations became a veritable celebration of the latest triumph of liberty over tyranny. Contemporary journals noted that the performances of *Brutus* at the Théâtre des Délassements Comiques would be embellished by the presence of Drouet and Guillaume, two of the heroes who had captured the fleeing king.

80. For Voltaire's apotheosis see Kellogg, Louise, 'Sur la translation des restes de Voltaire au Panthéon', *La Révolution française*, 37, 1899, pp. 271 f.; Dreyfous; Rockwood. The best contemporary accounts include the official program by Charron, Joseph, *Translation de Voltaire à Paris et détails de la cérémonie . . .*, Paris, undated [June 1791], and the reports

in the *Chronique de Paris, Le Courrier français* and *La Feuille villageoise.*
Thomas D. Kauffman's senior essay at Yale University (spring 1970)
largely refuted the interpretation of the apotheosis as a surrogate religion.

81. Wrongly attributed to David by most modern historians, including
Dreyfous, Rockwood and Dowd 1960. The *Moniteur* does say in its
account of the day that David 'furnished the drawings for the chariot',
but other writers simply give it to Célerier, and Charron, overseer of the
program says that Célerier took the idea of an antique chariot 'developed
and embellished it, and made the drawing of the chariot'. The best
modern account is in the special issue of the *Bulletin du Musée Carnavalet*
by Montgolfier, G. de, and Gallet, M., 'Souvenirs de Voltaire et de
Rousseau au Musée Carnavalet', 13 November 1960. Contemporary
descriptions agree on which inscriptions from Voltaire figured in the
ceremonies, but not on where they were used, some saying the chariot,
others referring to banners.

82. Those costumes and others modeled on the antique were probably designed by David. Contemporaries refer often to David's collaboration on the day's program. As the acknowledged head of radical artists,
he would have been consulted by Célerier and Charron.

83. *Détail exact et circonstancié de tous les objets relatifs à la fête de
Voltaire*, pamphlet extract published by the *Chronique de Paris*, July 1791.
The Voltaire hymn was published separately as *Hymn sur la translation
du corps de Voltaire.*

84. The emotional appeal of such a festival was a calculated one. Just
as contemporaries commented on how David's painting of *Brutus* moved
them to tears, so they wrote of the impact of the artfully contrived pro-
cessions. Mirabeau provided the defense for such appeals (Ar. Parl., 30,
entry for 10 September 1791. 'Discours sur l'éducation nationale', not
delivered in public but published in 1791; mentioned in Dowd 1948, p.
83). He proposed several festivals for each year, from which religion
would be excluded because it involves self-abnegation and the denial of
temporal emotions, and is therefore more appropriately confined to
churches. Greco-Roman festivals would instead be the model for the new
era devoted to 'the cult of liberty, the cult of law'. Man, he wrote, 'obeys
his impressions more than his reason.It is not enough to show him the
truth, the capital point is to make him passionate for her. It accomplishes
little to serve him in his immediate need, if one does not seize hold of his
imagination. It is a question less of convincing him than of moving him,
less of proving to him the excellence of the laws which govern him, than
to make him love them by means of his lively and emotional feelings . . .'

85. One month after the *Brutus* revival, the writer Laharpe published
a long manifesto, successor to Chénier's, on liberty in the theatre

('Liberté des théâtres', *Le Journal des amis de la constitution*, 4, 21 December 1790, pp. 171–83). It attacked the royal theatre for its monopoly hold on many plays, and also for its stubborn refusal to present *Brutus* until forced to. *Brutus* is 'this admirable tragedy whose only fault is to be above the century and the spectators, if only by virtue of these two verses where one says, speaking of a king, "And if he dares be false to the laws of Rome, / Rome is no more his subject, he alone is the rebel." It is the first time, perhaps, that one heard this word rebellious applied to a king. This word contains the whole doctrine, then so new and so little known among us, of the sovereignty of the nation.'

86. David Jules, pp. 109f. In addition to Dowd 1948, one should read descriptions of the festival in Mourey and in *Révolutions de Paris*, 4, 14–21 April 1792, pp. 97–108.

87. *Révolutions de Paris*, loc. cit., p. 101. In the same journal, p. 98, a crude engraving gives an imperfect idea of the William Tell subject.

88. Aulard Jacobins, 4, pp. 241f.

89. Ar. Parl., 49, entry for 1 September 1792. Here identified with the Assembly bust for the first time. Lossky, B., 'Oeuvres d'artistes néo-classiques peu connus au Musée de Tours', *BSHAF*, 1960, pp. 51–9, wrongly dates it *c.* 1795 and therefore excluded the connection. The base is inscribed: 'fait à Rome par F. J. Boiston citoyen du département du Doubs l'an 4 de la liberté'. 'Liberty' dated from 1789, and the more famous revolutionary years ('de la République') from September 1792, a source of frequent confusion.

90. Ar. Parl., 53–6, contain a rich documentation for the Convention debates, and all following citations are from its pages.

91. Bailly and other moderates had been saying in the same debates that killing a tyrant (Charles I, or Caesar) had always led to another tyrant, but that the banishment of Tarquin had been followed by an enduring republic. Sergent argues against banishment. Tarquin's exile is not a true analogy, he argued, because Rome's enemies were relatively weak and did not outmatch her, whereas France is surrounded by powerful kings. He then recapitulated the execution scene from the Brutus legend in such a way that demands for exile would be associated with anti-republican sentiment.

92. Bibliothèque Nationale, Cabinet des Estampes, 'Histoire de France', volume for January 1793.

93. *Feuille villageoise*, 18, 31 January 1793, pp. 429–31.

94. Rosenblum Transformations, p. 29.

95. Ar. Parl., 59, entry for 22 February 1793.

96. Ar. Parl., 59, entry for 6 March 1793.

97. *Discours prononcé à la Convention Nationale le 29 Mars 1793*, Imprimerie Nationale, 1793.

98. Ar. Parl., 49, documents the long and confused history of the re-building of the Tuileries theatre, although there is the excellent modern essay by Boyer, Ferdinand, 'Les Tuileries sous la Convention', *BSHAF*, 1934, pp. 197-241. By far the best contemporary account is that of the gifted historian Dulaure, J. A., in his *Thermomètre du jour*, 499, 13 May 1793, pp. 361-3.

99. Boyer identifies the artist as J. F. Strasbaux. Parker and others have thought they were actual statues.

100. Buchez Roux, 30, p. 84. Frenchmen almost carried the effigy of the first republican about in their pockets. On 23 May 1793 it was decreed that the heads of Brutus, Cato and Publicola would replace that of the king on assignats of 50, 15 and 10 sous. For unknown reasons, it was decided later that Justice, Abundance and Force would be more suitable.

101. Ar. Parl., 69, entry for 25 July 1793. On 6 August a bust of Marat by Deseine was also accepted, and presumably put in the Liberty Salon.

102. The Convention decreed on 2 August that for one month there be free public presentations of Voltaire's *Brutus*, Chénier's *Caïus Gracchus*, of *William Tell*, 'and other dramas which retrace the glorious events of the revolution and the virtues of the defenders of liberty'.

103. *Rapport et décret sur la Fête de la Réunion Républicaine du 10 Août*, Paris, 1793.

104. *Rapport fait . . . par David . . . pour l'explication de la médaille frappée en commémoration de la réunion civique de 10 Août 1792 . . .* The medal was made by Dupré.

105. Soboul has the best account of the cults of the martyrs.

106. *Sections de la Halle-au-bled et de Guillaume Tell réunies . . . pour l'inauguration des Bustes de Brutus, Michel Lepeletier et Paul Marat, Martyrs de la Liberté*, 6 October 1793, and Palloy, *Adresse aux sections de la Halle-au-Bled et Guillaume Tell*, 15 October 1793.

107. The painting has been well served in Lankeit, but needs to be supplemented by contemporary accounts. The best for this October ceremony are *Section du Museum; Ordre de la marche; Pompe funèbre . . . pour l'inauguration des bustes de Marat et de Lepeletier*, 16 October 1793, and *Exposition dans la cour du Louvre des tableaux de Lepeletier et de Marat* of the same date. The reliable Lenoir referred to the Louvre exhibition of the two pictures as a 'chapelle ardente'.

108. John Gage has pointed out the possible connection of *Marat* with Pigalle's *Tomb of Comte Henri-Claude d'Honcourt* (St-Severin) of the 1770s. The cadaverous effigy is shown half-risen from its open sarco-

phagus, so like Marat's tub. Comparison with sarcophagi is aided by David's treatment of the tub. In reality it sloped down from the open end, like a giant slipper, but David hid this form under the horizontal of his invented drapery.

109. *Section de Brutus, Adresse présentée à la Convention Nationale . . .*, 19 April 1794.

110. Ar. Parl., 82, entry for 25 December 1793.

111. *Liberté, Egalité, Fraternité. Gendarmerie nationale servant près des Tribunaux. Procès-verbal de l'inauguration des bustes de Brutus, Marat, Lepeletier*, 20 November 1793.

112. Biré, Edmond, 'La Révolution et l'enfance', *Revue de la Révolution*, 1, 1883, pp. 64-91.

113. *Moniteur*, 154, 4 Ventose l'an 2 [22 February 1794], p. 531.

114. Aulard Salut, 7, 8, 9, *passim*, and Soboul, pp. 282ff.

115. D'Estrée, p. 50.

116. Dieudonné, F., 'La déchristianisation de la commune de Ris-Orangis', *La Révolution française*, 44, 14 June 1903, pp. 508-17. See also Figuères, Roger de, *Les noms révolutionnaires des communes de France*, Paris, 1901. Such village festivals had their charm: 'On the chariot was Liberty, below which were Reason and Equality represented by the *citoyennes* Mien and Bezeaut. Victory held the bust of Brutus being crowned by a genie . . .Arriving at the monument where the bust of Brutus was to be placed, the chariot stopped, this great man was installed on the monument, the oath was pronounced . . .'

117. Aulard Art, pp. 262ff, recorded David's descriptions of the caricatures but not that they had survived. Both are documented most fully in Blum, André, *La Caricature Révolutionnaire 1789 à 1795*, Paris, 1916, pp. 195f. *The Army of Jugs* was loosely etched by Jaime, E., *Musée de la Caricature*, vol. 2, Paris, 1838, pl. 54G, without knowing David was the artist. His collaborator P. Chasles was enthusiastic over a work which reminded him of 'a rough sketch by a school child on vacation', and he appreciated the artist's graphic rendering of the *sans-culottes* on the archway: 'l'auteur a tiré un parti ultra-poétique du mot sans-culotte, qu'il a réduit à sa valeur matérielle'. Jug in French is *cruche*, which also means dolt or blockhead. Pitt is shown as the turkey who is master of the king; Fox is the goose, master of the people. The syringe-canons to the rear are being filled as unavailing weapons against the Constitution. For the other [55], David's text says in part: 'the government is represented in the form of a devil flayed alive, monopolizing commerce and covered with all the royal decorations. The portrait of the king is found on the backside of the government which vomits on its people a multitude of taxes . . .'

118. *Rapport fait au nom du Comité d'instruction publique par David sur la nomination des cinquante membres du Jury . . .* 25 Brumaire l'an 2 [15 November 1793].

119. *Rapport fait à la Convention Nationale par David*, 27 Brumaire l'an 2 [17 November 1793], p. 4. This report confirmed a proposal David had made in the Convention on the 17th Brumaire.

120. *Ordre, marche et cérémonies de la Fête à l'Être Suprême qui doit être célébrée le 20 Prairial d'après le plan proposé par David . . . .* undated [1793].

121. 'Sur les rapports des idées religieuses et morales avec les principes républicains . . .', published separately as a broadside and in *Journal des débats*, 596, pp. 239-59.

122. None the less there was more continuity than generally acknowledged. For example, the *Leonidas* (Louvre) which he worked on throughout the Napoleonic period not only corresponds to the *Horatii* in the choice of the moment before battle, it also embodies the patriotic aspirations of the early Revolution. In 1789, after saying that 'we should not forget in this revolution the powerful effect of the language of signs', the *Révolutions de Paris*, 1, 5-12 September, p. 26, wrote: 'The Spartans elevated in the pass of Thermopylae a monument to these 300 brave citizens . . . with this simple inscription: *passer-by, go tell Sparta that we are here to obey its sacred laws.* Never does an inhabitant of Greece pass this place without feeling a religious tremor which elevates his soul to the point that he envies the fate of these heroes, and without swearing an eternal hate to tyrants.'

123. The play seems not to have been put on in the winter and spring of 1794, and after Thermidor, Grégoire accused the Robespierre government of interdicting it because of its lines opposing arbitrary arrest and favoring careful legal procedures (Aulard Directoire, 1, p. 316). Proof of the association of the play with forces opposing the Jacobin dictatorship is offered by the Thermidorean theatre: from August through December, Voltaire's play was suddenly revived and given repeatedly, mostly at the Gaieté. After 1794, the play rapidly waned and its last performance in Paris was in the summer of 1799. In the same year there was also one of the last memorable uses of lines from the play for the purposes of public exhortation. A commemoration of the execution of Louis XVI was celebrated at the 'Temple of Victory' (St-Sulpice). After a giant military parade during which the 'oath of hatred' was sworn against 'royalty and anarchy', the participants came to the erstwhile church, whose façade was decorated with two gigantic inscriptions. One recalled that the execution had been a 'day of fear for traitors and perjurers', and the other

cited the often quoted lines, with the customary alterations, 'If in the Republic there be a traitor,/Who laments the king or who wishes a master,/May he die a death full of tortures, . . .' (Aulard Directoire, 5, pp. 330–33).

124. The touch of deep tragedy in the Brutus theme had a curious heritage in the nineteenth century, kindly pointed out to me by Douglas Schoenherr. The American J. H. Payne wrote his play *Brutus* in 1818 (basing it on a play of 1813 by Richard Cumberland), and it toured the midwest with the actor of appropriate name Lucius Junius Booth, who had been so christened in 1796. It was one of the sons of Lucius Junius Booth who shot Lincoln in the theatre in Washington.

125. Hennin, Michel, *Histoire numismatique de la Révolution française*, Paris, 1826, p. 75; Boppe, Auguste, *Les Vignettes emblématiques sous la Révolution*, Paris, 1911, *passim*.

126. Boyer, Ferdinand, 'Six statues de législateurs antiques pour le Palais-Bourbon sous le Directoire', *BSHAF*, 1958, pp. 91–4.

127. Montaiglon, Anatole de (ed.), *Correspondance des Directeurs de l'Académie de France à Rome avec les Surintendants des Bâtiments*, Paris, 1887; 16, p. 419. The importance the French gave to these works of art was shown by assigning the trouble-shooter and roving legate Comte Miot to oversee the negotiations: Comte André François Miot de Mélito, *Mémoires* (ed. by W. de Fleischmann), Paris, 1858, 1, *passim*. A sketch of Miot by Louis Gauffier (Musée de Versailles) dating from this time shows the legate and his family next to a seated statue of the French Republic and a larger-than-life copy after the Capitoline Brutus.

128. The festival, organized by the architect Chalgrin, is described in the anonymous *Fêtes de la Liberté et entrée triomphale des objets des sciences et des arts recueillis en Italie*, Paris, 1798, and among others, in the *Moniteur*, 309, 9 Thermidor l'an 6 [27 July 1798], pp. 322–4.

129. Aulard Consulat, 1, p. 93. Napoleon's associations with antiquity are brilliantly summarized in Bertrand, p. 322 and *passim*.

130. In a separate publication I will deal with Napoleon and Henri IV. Baron Gros took the principal elements of his *Napoleon at Eylau* (Louvre) from Gravelot's engraving of Henri IV for Voltaire's *Henriade*.

131. In 1830 G. S. Andrieux published his tragedy *Lucius Junius Brutus*, which he had begun during the great Revolution. The half-title page reads: 'Vittorio Alfieri a dédié sa Tragédie de *Brutus* "Al Popolo Italiano Libero Futuro", Au peuple italien qui deviendra libre. Je dédie la mienne: Au Peuple Français Devenu Libre.' The long preface is a fascinating account of the gestation of this later play (at one time read to a group including the painter Gérard), and of the literary history of the legend of Brutus.

Bibliography

Adhémar Calques: Adhémar, Jean and Armingent, J., *David, naissance du génie d'un peintre*, Monte Carlo, 1953. Album of David tracings.

Andrieux, G. S., *Lucius Junius Brutus*, Paris, 1830.

Ar. Parl.: *Archives parlementaires de 1787 à 1860*, Paris, 82 vols., 1862–1913.

Aulard Art: Aulard, F. A., 'L'Art et la politique en l'an II', *Etudes et leçons sur la Révolution française*, I, 1893, pp. 241–67.

Aulard Consulat: —, *Paris sous le Consulat*, Paris, 4 vols., 1903–9.

Aulard Directoire: —, *Paris pendant la réaction thermidorienne et sous le Directoire*, Paris, 5 vols., 1898–1902.

Aulard Histoire: —, *Histoire politique de la Révolution française*, Paris, 1901.

Aulard Jacobins: —, *La Société des Jacobins . . .*, Paris, 6 vols., 1889–97.

Aulard Salut: —, *Recueil des actes du Comité de Salut Public*, Paris, 28 vols., 1889–1955.

Berezina, Valentina N., *Jacques-Louis David*, Leningrad, 1963.

Bertrand: Bertrand, Louis, *La fin du classicisme et le retour à l'antique dans la seconde moitié du XVIIIe siècle . . .*, Paris, 1897. Superb study, Locquin's spiritual guide.

Boyer, Ferdinand, 'Les Tuileries sous la Convention', *BSHAF*, 1934, pp. 197–241.

—, 'Six statues de législateurs antiques pour le Palais-Bourbon sous le Directoire', *BSHAF*, 1958, pp. 91–4.

—, *Le Monde des arts en Italie et la France de la Révolution et de l'Empire*, Turin, 1970.

Buchez Roux: Buchez, P. J. B. and Roux, P. C., *Histoire parlementaire de la Révolution française*, Paris, 40 vols., 1834–8.

Carlson, Marvin, *The Theater of the French Revolution*, Cornell University, 1967.

Caubisens-Lesfargues, Colette, 'Le Salon de peinture pendant la Révolution', *Annales historiques de la Révolution française*, 33, April–June 1961, pp. 191–214.

Charron, Joseph: *Translation de Voltaire à Paris . . .*, Paris, n.d. [1791].

Chénier, M. J.: *De la liberté du théâtre en France*, Paris, 1789.

Coggins, Clemency, 'Tracings in the work of Jacques-Louis David', *Gazette des Beaux-Arts*, 6, 72, November 1968, pp. 259–64.

Correspondance: Furcy-Raynaud, M., ed., 'Correspondance de M. d'Angiviller avec Pierre', *Nouvelles archives de l'art français*, vols. 20 and 22, 1906.

Crozet: Crozet, René, 'David et l'architecture Néo-classique', *Gazette des Beaux-Arts*, 6 April 1955, pp. 211-20.

David Jules: David, J. L. Jules, *Le peintre Louis David, 1748-1825, souvenir et documents inédits*, Paris, 1880. Still indispensable, especially for republished documents.

Delécluze, Etienne J., *Louis David, son école et son temps*, Paris, 1855.

Deloynes, *Collection Deloynes*, multi-volume anthology (partly hand-written) of criticism of the eighteenth and early nineteenth centuries, in the Cabinet des Estampes, Bibliothèque Nationale, Paris.

D'Estrée, Paul [i.e., Quentin, Henri], *Le théâtre sous la terreur*, Paris, 1913.

Dowd 1948: Dowd, David Lloyd, *Pageant Master of the Republic; Jacques-Louis David and the Revolution*, University of Nebraska, 1948. Careful study of David's public role, with a superb critical bibliography.

Dowd 1960: __, 'Art and the theater during the French Revolution: the role of Louis David', *Art Quarterly*, 23, Spring 1960, pp. 3-22.

__, 'Jacobinism and the fine arts: the Revolutionary careers of Bouquier, Sergent and David', *Art Quarterly*, 16, Autumn 1953, pp. 195-214.

Dreyfous: Dreyfous, Maurice, *Les Arts et les artistes pendant la période révolutionnaire . . .*, Paris, 1906.

Engerand: Engerand, Fernand, *Inventaire des tableaux commandés et achetés par la Direction des Bâtiments du Roi (1709-1792)*, Paris, 1900.

Ettlinger: Ettlinger, Leopold, 'Jacques-Louis David and Roman Virtue', *Journal of the Royal Society of Arts*, 115, January 1967, pp. 105-23.

Grimm: Grimm, Friedrich Melchior Von, and Diderot, Denis (Tourneux, Maurice, ed.), *Correspondance littéraire, philosophique et critique par Grimm, Diderot . . .*, Paris, 16 vols., 1877-82.

Hautecoeur: Hautecoeur, Louis, *Louis David*, Paris, 1954. Essentially derivative, but the best modern biography.

Holma: Holma, Klaus, *David, son évolution et son style*, Paris, 1940. Frequently wrongheaded, but provocative.

Honour: Honour, Hugh, *Neo-classicism*, Harmondsworth, 1968. The best general study of the subject.

Joannidès, A., *La Comédie Française de 1680 à 1900*, Paris, 1901; expanded in *La Comédie Française de 1680 à 1900, tableau des représentations*, Paris, 1921.

Kellogg, Louise, 'Mémoire d'une étudiante américaine sur la translation des restes de Voltaire au Panthéon le 11 Juillet 1791', *La Révolution française*, 37, 14 September 1899, pp. 271-7. The essential early study of the 1791 apotheosis.

Lankheit: Lankheit, Klaus, *Der Tod Marats*, Stuttgart, 1961.

Lee, Virginia, 'Jacques-Louis David: the Versailles sketchbook', *Burlington Magazine*, 111, April 1969, pp. 197-208, and June 1969, pp. 360-69.

Lefebvre: Lefebvre, Georges, *The Coming of the French Revolution* (translated by R. R. Palmer), Princeton, 1947 [1939].

Leith, James A., *The Idea of Art as Propaganda in France 1750-1799*, University of Toronto, 1965. Deals with largely obvious issues in a general survey.

Lenoir: Lenoir, Alexandre, 'David, souvenirs historiques', *Journal de l'Institut historique*, 2, August 1835, pp. 1-13.

Locquin: Locquin, Jean, *La peinture d'histoire en France de 1747 à 1785*, Paris, 1912. One of the great books in art history.

Mathiez: Mathiez, Albert, *Les Origines des cultes révolutionnaires, 1789-1792*, Paris, 1904.

McKee: McKee, Kenneth N., 'Voltaire's *Brutus* during the French Revolution', *Modern Language Notes*, 56, 1941, pp. 100-6.

Montgolfier, Bernard de, and Gallet, Michel, 'Souvenirs de Voltaire et de Rousseau au Musée Carnavalet', *Bulletin du Musée Carnavalet*, 13 November 1960. Special issue on the subject, marvelously documented.

Mourey: Mourey, Gabriel, *Le Livre des fêtes françaises*, Paris, 1930.

Notice: Anonymous [probably Thomé de Gamond, Aimé], *Notice sur la vie et les ouvrages de M. J. L. David*, Paris, 1824.

Parker: Parker, Harold T., *The Cult of Antiquity and the French Revolutionaries*, Chicago, 1937. Includes the best summary of the cult of Brutus.

Renouvier: Renouvier, Jules, *Histoire de l'art pendant la Révolution considéré principalement dans les estampes*, Paris, 2 vols., 1863. The monumental study of prints and printmakers, with biographies and iconographical analyses.

Ridgway: Ridgway, Ronald S., 'La propagande philosophique dans les tragédies de Voltaire', *Studies on Voltaire and the 18th Century*, XV, 1961, pp. 71-89.

Rockwood: Rockwood, Raymond O., *The Cult of Voltaire to 1791*, unpublished dissertation, University of Chicago, 1935, and 'The Legend of Voltaire and the cult of the Revolution, 1791', *Ideas in History, Essays presented to Louis Gottschalk* (Richard Herr, ed.), Durham, North Carolina, 1965, pp. 110-34.

Rosenblum Transformations: Rosenblum, Robert, *Transformations in late Eighteenth-Century Art*, Princeton, 1967. Wonderfully inventive analysis of major iconographical themes.

—, 'A source for David's "Horatii"', *Burlington Magazine*, 112, May 1970, pp. 269–73.

Rosenthal: Rosenthal, Léon, *Louis David*, Paris, 1905.

Sagnac, Philippe, and Robiquet, Jean, *La Révolution de 1789*, Paris, 2 vols., 1934 [i.e., 1938]. The best pictorial repertoire.

Saunier: Saunier, Charles, 'Voyage de David à Nantes en 1790', *Revue de l'art ancien et moderne*, 14, July 1903, pp. 33–41.

Sloane, Joseph C., 'David, Robespierre and "The Death of Bara"', *Gazette des Beaux-Arts*, 6, 74, September 1969, pp. 143–57.

Soboul: Soboul, Albert, *Les Sans-culottes parisiens en l'an II*, Paris, 1958. Masterful study with rich bibliographies.

Von Halem: Von Halem, G. A., *Paris en 1790* (translated and edited by A. Chuquet), Paris, 1896. One of the best witness accounts.

Wille: Wille, J. G., *Mémoires et journal de J. G. Wille, graveur du Roi* (Georges Duplessis ed.), Paris, 2 vols., 1857.

List of Illustrations

Color plate: *Lictors Returning to Brutus the Bodies of his Sons.* By David, 1789. Oil on Canvas, 325 x 423 cm. Paris, Louvre. (Photo: Giraudon.)

1. *The Oath of the Horatii.* By David, 1784-5. Oil on canvas. Paris, Louvre. (Photo: Bulloz.)

2. *Brutus and Members of his Household.* By David, c. 1788. Black chalk, 14.4 x 19.2 cm. Bayonne, Musée Bonnat. (Photo: Archives photographiques.)

3. *The Dejected Brutus.* By David, c. 1788. Black chalk, 14.3 x 10.5 cm. Bayonne, Musée Bonnat. (Photo: Archives photographiques.)

4. Compositional study for *Brutus.* By David, c. 1788. Brown chalk, 23 x 31 cm. Courtesy the Robert Lehman Collection, New York. (Photo: Lehman Collection.)

5. *Brutus's Wife and Daughters.* By David, c. 1788. Black chalk, 25.8 x 35.5 cm. Paris, Louvre. (Photo: Réunion des Musées Nationaux.)

6. Illustration for Voltaire's *Irène.* Engraving by Moreau-le-Jeune and LeMire, published 1786. Paris, Bibliothèque Nationale. (Photo: Bibliothèque Nationale.)

7. Compositional study for *Brutus.* By David, c. 1788. Black chalk, 21.5 x 33.5 cm. Bayonne, Musée Bonnat. (Photo: Archives Photographiques.)

8. *Brutus seated, head erect.* By David, c. 1788. Black chalk, 14.3 x 11.1 cm. Bayonne, Musée Bonnat. (Photo: Archives Photographiques.)

9. Study for *Weeping Servant.* By David, c. 1788. Black chalk, fragment of larger sheet. Paris, Louvre. (Photo: Réunion des Musées Nationaux.)

10. Oil study for *Brutus.* By David, c. 1788. Oil on canvas, 28 x 36 cm. Stockholm, National Museum. (Photo: Museum.)

11. *The Fainting Daughter.* By David, 1789. Ink, 10.7 x 11.5 cm. Paris, Fondation Custodia. (Photo: Fondation Custodia.)

12. *Skirt and foot of Brutus's wife.* By David, c. 1789. Black crayon, fragment of larger sheet. Paris, Louvre. (Photo: Réunion des Musées Nationaux.)

13. *The Weeping Servant.* By David, 1789. Black and white chalks, 56.6 x 43.2 cm. Tours, Musée des Beaux-Arts. (Photo: Museum.)

14. Detail of *Brutus.* (Photo: Réunion des Musées Nationaux.)

15. The Capitoline *Brutus*. Roman sculpture. Bronze. Rome, Vatican. (Photo: Anderson-Viollet.)

16. Tracing after the Capitoline *Brutus*. By David, *c.* 1784? Ink, 22 x 16.5 cm. Collection unknown. (Photo: Yale University Library.)

17. Detail of *Brutus*. (Photo: Giraudon.)

18. Detail from Niobid Sarcophagus. Roman sculpture. Marble. Rome, Lateran Museum. (Photo: Alinari.)

19. Detail from Niobid Sarcophagus. Roman sculpture. Marble. Rome, Vatican. (Photo: Alinari.)

20. *Seated Philosopher*. Roman sculpture. Marble. Rome, Palazzo Spada. (Photo: Mansell-Alinari.)

21. Detail of *Brutus*. (Photo: Réunion des Musées Nationaux.)

22. *Jupiter*, detail from tracing. By David, *c.* 1784? Ink, 14 x 26 cm. Collection unknown. (Photo: Yale University Library.)

23. *Isaiah* from the Sistine Ceiling. By Michelangelo. Fresco. Rome, Vatican. (Photo: Alinari.)

24. *Death of Socrates*. By J. F. P. Peyron, 1790. Engraving. Paris, Bibliothèque Nationale. (Photo: Bibliothèque Nationale.)

25. Roman wall decoration from Herculaneum. Engraving by F. Cepparoli after N. Vanni, 1762, in *Le pitture antiche d'Ercolano*, vol. 3. (Photo: Yale University Library.)

26. Detail of *Brutus*. (Photo: Giraudon.)

27. Detail of *Brutus*. (Photo: Giraudon.)

28. *The Salon of 1789*, detail. By Charles de Wailly, 1789. Drawing, mixed techniques. Paris, Musée Carnavalet. (Photo: the author.)

29. *Lavoisier and his Wife*. By David, 1788. Oil on canvas. New York, Rockefeller University. (Photo: Bulloz.)

30. *Lally-Tollendal Unveiling the Bust of his Father*. By J. B. C. Robin, 1787. Oil on canvas. New York, Walter P. Chrysler, Jr. (Photo: Oliver Baker.)

31. *Demolition of the Bastille*. By Hubert Robert, 1789. Oil on canvas. Paris, Musée Carnavalet. (Photo: Bulloz.)

32. *The Bastille Escapee Henri Masers de Latude*. By Antoine Vestier, 1789. Oil on canvas. Paris, Musée Carnavalet. (Photo: Bulloz.)

33. The head of *Brutus*. By David, 1790. Black crayon, 28.6 x 22.2 cm. (sight). New York, Mrs Elizabeth M. Drey. (Photo: John D. Shiff.)

34. *Oath in the Tennis Court*. By David, 1790-91. Drawing, mixed techniques. Paris, Louvre. (Photo: Bulloz.)

35. *Altar to the Fatherland.* Anonymous engraving, 1790, in *Révolutions de France et de Brabant*, vol. 44 (September). (Photo: Yale University Library.)

36. *Portrait of Mirabeau.* Artist unknown. Oil on canvas. London, The Duke of Hamilton. (Photo: A. C. Cooper.)

37. *Voltaire Honored at the Revival of Brutus.* Anonymous engraving, 1790, in *Révolutions de France et de Brabant*, vol. 53 (December). (Photo: Yale University Library.)

38. Illustration for Voltaire's *Brutus.* Engraving by Alexandre Desenne, in *Oeuvres Complètes de Voltaire*, 1826. (Photo: Harlingue-Viollet.)

39. Chariot design for Apotheosis of Voltaire. By Jacques Célerier, 1791. Pencil. Paris, Musée Carnavalet. (Photo: Bulloz.)

40. *Voltaire's Remains Transported to the Panthéon.* By C. Malapeau and S. Miger, 1791. Etching and engraving. Paris, Bibliothèque Nationale. (Photo: Bibliothèque Nationale.)

41. Sash commemorating Voltaire's Apotheosis. Anonymous, 1791. Cloth. Paris, Musée Carnavalet. (Photo: Bulloz.)

42. *Festival of Liberty for the Soldiers of Châteauvieux, 15 April 1792*, detail. Engraving by P. G. Berthault after J. L. Prieur. Paris, Bibliothèque Nationale. (Photo: Giraudon.)

43. *Storming of the Tuileries, 10 August 1792.* By J. Duplessis-Bertaux, 1792. Versailles, Musée. (Photo: Bulloz.)

44. *Lucius Junius Brutus.* By Joseph Boiston, 1792. Marble, 86 cm. high. Tours, Musée des Beaux-Arts. (Photo: J. J. Moreau.)

45. *Exposition of Lepeletier's Body.* Anonymous engraving, 1793, in *Révolutions de Paris*, vol. 15 (January). (Photo: Yale University Library.)

46. *Ferraud Assassinated in the Convention, 1795*, detail. Engraving by J. Duplessis-Bertaux. Paris, Bibliothèque Nationale. (Photo: Bibliothèque Nationale.)

47. *Liberty and Equality united by Nature.* Engraving by L. C. Ruotte, *c.* 1793. Paris, Musée Carnavalet. (Photo: the author.)

48. Lepeletier, Marat, Chalier, *Martyrs to Liberty.* Anonymous engraving, *c.* 1793. Paris, Musée Carnavalet. (Photo: Bulloz.)

49. *Marat.* By David, 1793. Oil on canvas. Brussels, Musées Royaux. (Photo: Bulloz.)

50. *Royalty Annihilated.* Anonymous broadside, *c.* 1794. Paris, Musée Carnavalet. (Photo: the author.)

51. *Brutus.* Engraving by J. B. Vérité, *c.* 1794. Paris, Bibliothèque Nationale. (Photo: Bibliothèque Nationale.)

52. *Brutus* and *Marat.* Anonymous engravings, *c.* 1793-4. Paris, Musée Carnavalet. (Photo: the author.)

53. Playing Cards of the Revolution. Woodcuts by J. Minot, 1794. Paris, Bibliothèque Nationale. (Photo: Bibliothèque Nationale.)

54. *The Army of Jugs.* Colored broadside by David, published by Bance, 1794. Paris, Bibliothèque Nationale. (Photo: Bibliothèque Nationale.)

55. *The English Government.* Colored broadside by David, published by Bance, 1794. Paris, Bibliothèque Nationale. (Photo: Bibliothèque Nationale.)

56. *Triumph of the People.* By David, *c.* 1793-4. Drawing, mixed techniques. Paris, Musée Carnavalet. (Photo: Bulloz.)

57. Brutus, detail from *Triumph of the People.* (Photo: the author.)

58. *Voltaire and Rousseau Honoring the Supreme Being.* Anonymous broadside, 1794. Paris, Musée Carnavalet. (Photo: the author.)

59. *Louis XVI separated from his Family.* Engraving by J. B. Vérité after P. Bouillon, 1794. Paris, Musée Carnavalet. (Photo: Bulloz.)

60. *Brutus.* Engraving by P. Audouin after Molenchon, 1794-5. Paris, Bibliothèque Nationale. (Photo: Bibliothèque Nationale.)

61. *Brutus.* Engraving by L. Darcis after Guillon Lethière, *c.* 1795-6. Paris, Bibliothèque Nationale. (Photo: Bibliothèque Nationale.)

62. *Brutus.* By Frédéric Lemot, 1798. Plaster. Paris, Chambre des Députés. (Photo: Bulloz.)

Index

[Note: Works of art are referred to by bold numbers; *n.* and *ns.* are note numbers. Works of art central to this study are entered separately, under their authors' names. Surnames are used except where confusion might result.]